Messages from
Your Angels

Audio/CD Programs

ANGEL MEDICINE: A Healing Meditation CD (available October 2004)

ANGELS AMONG US (with Michael Toms)

MESSAGES FROM YOUR ANGELS (abridged audio book)

PAST-LIFE REGRESSION WITH THE ANGELS

DIVINE PRESCRIPTIONS

THE ROMANCE ANGELS

CONNECTING WITH YOUR ANGELS

MANIFESTING WITH THE ANGELS

KARMA RELEASING

HEALING YOUR APPETITE, HEALING YOUR LIFE

HEALING WITH THE ANGELS

DIVINE GUIDANCE

CHAKRA CLEARING

Oracle Cards

(44 or 45 divination cards and guidebook)

HEALING WITH THE ANGELS ORACLE CARDS

HEALING WITH THE FAIRIES ORACLE CARDS

MESSAGES FROM YOUR ANGELS ORACLE CARDS (card deck and booklet)

MAGICAL MERMAIDS AND DOLPHINS ORACLE CARDS (card deck and booklet)

ARCHANGEL ORACLE CARDS (card deck and booklet)

GODDESS GUIDANCE ORACLE CARDS (card deck and booklet)

MAGICAL UNICORNS ORACLE CARDS (available April 2005)

All of the above are available at your local bookstore, or may be ordered by visiting: Hay House USA: **www.hayhouse.com**; Hay House Australia: **www.hayhouse.com.au**; Hay House UK: **www.hayhouse.co.uk**; Hay House South Africa: **orders@psdprom.co.za**

Doreen's Website: **www.AngelTherapy.com**

Messages from Your Angels

What Your Angels Want You to Know

HAY HOUSE, INC.
Carlsbad, California
London • Sydney • Johannesburg
Vancouver • Hong Kong

Copyright © 2002 by Doreen Virtue

Published and distributed in the United States by: Hay House, Inc., P.O. Box 5100, Carlsbad, CA 92018-5100 • *Phone:* (760) 431-7695 or (800) 654-5126 • *Fax:* (760) 431-6948 or (800) 650-5115 • www.hayhouse.com • **Published and distributed in Australia by:** Hay House Australia Pty. Ltd., 18/36 Ralph St., Alexandria NSW 2015 • *Phone:* 612-9669-4299 • *Fax:* 612-9669-4144 • www.hayhouse.com.au • **Published and distributed in the United Kingdom by:** Hay House UK, Ltd. • Unit 62, Canalot Studios • 222 Kensal Rd., London W10 5BN • *Phone:* 44-20-8962-1230 • *Fax:* 44-20-8962-1239 • www.hayhouse.co.uk • **Published and distributed in the Republic of South Africa by:** Hay House SA (Pty), Ltd., P.O. Box 990, Witkoppen 2068 • *Phone/Fax:* 2711-7012233 • orders@psdprom.co.za • **Distributed in Canada by:** Raincoast • 9050 Shaughnessy St., Vancouver, B.C. V6P 6E5 • *Phone:* (604) 323-7100 • *Fax:* (604) 323-2600

Editorial supervision: Jill Kramer • *Design:* Jenny Richards

Library of Congress Cataloging-in-Publication Data

Virtue, Doreen.
    Messages from your angels : what your angels want you to know / Doreen Virtue.
        p. cm.
    ISBN 1-56170-860-7 (hardcover) • 1-4019-0049-6 (tradepaper)
    1. Spirit writings. 2. Angels--Miscellanea. I. Title.
BF1290 .V57 2002
133.9'3--dc21

                                                          2002001460

ISBN 1-4019-0049-6

07 06 05 04   14 13 12 11
1st printing, April 2002
14th printing, June 2004

Printed in the United States of America

Contents

Introduction
by Doreen Virtue

This is the sequel to *Angel Therapy*, a book that changed my life during its writing and creation. However, it is *not* necessary to first read *Angel Therapy* to understand, or receive, the full benefits from this book. *Messages with Your Angels* stands alone.

On the day that I conceived the idea to write *Angel Therapy*, I sent a one-sentence e-mail message to my publisher, Hay House, telling them about it. Normally, a publisher asks to see a detailed proposal before they agree to publish a book. But amazingly, within hours, Hay House agreed to publish *Angel Therapy* even though I hadn't sent them much more than a book title. I wouldn't have been able to send them a description of the book in any case—I had no idea what it was going to be about! The angels were clearly guiding and directing the process from above, and my publisher and I were influenced by them.

The first half of *Angel Therapy* was dictated to me by the angels. I'd sit at my computer, pray, and then go into a semi-trance. It seemed like the angels' words bypassed my conscious awareness and went directly to my fingers typing on the keyboard. I was concerned that the words might be unintelligible, so I hesitated to read the manuscript until it was complete. It was only then that I discovered the angels' sweet and wise guidance, which comprises the first half of *Angel Therapy*. I learned so much from their words, yet some of their messages were "above" my level of spiritual understanding at that time—not superior to it, but just coming from a higher spiritual consciousness than I possessed. Over time, I gradually understood what the angels were saying, and today, their messages make so much sense to me!

Writing this book, *Messages from Your Angels*, was entirely different. Several years have passed since I wrote *Angel Therapy*, and I've been criss-crossing the world, giving workshops in which I publicly channel the angels. As a result, I'm much more comfortable with, and accustomed to, the process.

Just like *Angel Therapy*, *Messages from Your Angels* was dictated to me by the angels after I prayed for their guidance. They chose the topics for Part I of this book, and they told me exactly what to write. Each chapter contains material that surprised me when I read it, as this was new information to me in most cases. The angels' logic is amazingly clear, yet refreshingly different from the mortal mind. So, once again, I learned a great deal as the scribe of the angels' communications.

In Part II, I asked the angels a number of questions—many of which I'm frequently asked by audience members, and some that are queries of my own. In this Part, the angels started to respond to me as soon as I mentally asked them the particular question, but sometimes their timing was a little inconvenient for me. For instance, one time when I was jogging through an oceanfront park in La Jolla, California, I decided to ask the angels about the nature and purpose of dolphins. It was no sooner than I mentally posed that question that I heard the angels' wry reply (which you'll read later). I appealed to the angels to "Hold that thought!" until I could return to the laptop computer in my hotel room to type their message.

The same scenario repeated itself during several jogging sessions. However, after the angels "wrote" the chapter on "Breath" (the chapters weren't completed in chronological order), I better understood their method. According to the angels, their messages are partially carried to us on oxygen molecules, so the more we breathe, and the higher the quality of air that we take in, the more clear their messages are to us. While jogging, of course, my breath was deeper and faster—and so were my angelic messages. When I'm in locations that have better air quality, I notice that my angelic communications and angel readings are more detailed and clear.

The Process

The process I went through in order to write this book was to sit at my computer, take a few deep breaths, close my eyes, and pray for Heaven to write through me. My prayers reflect my metaphysical Christian background, although these writings are definitely nondenominational and apply to those from all religious and nonreligious backgrounds.

After praying, I'd focus on a topic or question and ask the angels to write that section through me. That's when I'd hear a gentle but firm voice in my right ear that had a distinctly male quality to its tone and energy. This communication emanated from Archangel Michael, as well as a group of angels who simply call themselves "The Angelic Realm." They're "spokes-angels," if you will.

The voice dictated the words to me, and it corrected me when I misheard it. It told me when to italicize a word and when to put a phrase in quotes. When I would ask the voice, "Are you sure about this particular phrasing?" it would firmly tell me, "Yes, leave it as is," or it would correct words that I'd taken down wrong as a result of mishearing the dictation.

As a former psychotherapist, I was taught throughout my university training to be a professional skeptic. It's a basic foundation of psychology to read pathology into anything that defies the material senses. So, when I first began to engage in this form of automatic writing, it was natural for me to doubt its validity.

I became convinced of its authenticity for two reasons. First, there was the voice's distinctly male quality. If I'd been making up these words, surely it would come through a female voice, and probably a voice that sounded like my own. That's not to say that, if you hear a voice in your own gender, it's your imagination. However, when the voice is from a different gender, it's much easier to distinguish it from mere imagination.

Second, each time that I automatically wrote, I would learn new material that I'd never before read, heard, or thought about! This is what convinced me most that these writings were authentic. I found it very exciting to sit at the computer each time, knowing that I would access fresh information! I'd approach my writing sessions and wonder, *What will I learn today?*

So judge for yourself, please, as you read the angels' channelings. Your mind, heart, and feelings will tell you whether they're authentic or not.

When I was an undergraduate, I minored in philosophy, and I took a few courses on logic and rhetoric. Those courses inspired me to analyze the underlying rationale in presentations. It's one reason why the angels' logic within their writings is remarkable to me. They present new viewpoints that—once you grasp them—seem so reasonable. It made me wonder, *Why didn't I realize that before?* I find that their way of looking at humanity and life is very clear, and it gives us humans a lot more credit than we give ourselves.

Working and talking with the angels is much more of an integral part of my life now than when I wrote *Angel Therapy*. It's much easier for me to "remember" to ask them to help me with all parts of my life, and they always come through! I'm noticing this same positive trend with my workshop attendees. Increasingly, people from corporate or traditional religious backgrounds are in attendance. There's a new openness to spirituality, devoid of paranoia or guilt, which is utterly refreshing! I find that the audience members are pragmatic, independent-minded people who simply want to explore different avenues of spirituality for themselves. They want to experiment and make up their own minds about spirituality, instead of having some authoritative religious figure tell them what to do or how to pray. This reflects the very underlying freedom of Spirit, don't you agree?

We All Hear the Angels

We all hear the voice of Heaven—I believe this with all my heart. The voice comes through our heart, our gut, our head, our ears, and our eyes. It influences far more than we know—but only when we give it permission to through our formal or casual prayers. Even a rhetorical cry for help, such as, "If anyone can hear me, please help!" is enough to evoke our angels' assistance.

My mission hasn't been so much to help people hear their angels as it is to create an atmosphere where we're less afraid of acknowledging and following their guidance. In nearly every angel reading I give, my client will say something like, "That's what I *thought* my angels were trying to tell me!" I'm merely there to validate the guidance they've already absorbed, and perhaps act as a catalyst for them to follow that guidance.

Yet, fear clouds this process. There are fears ranging from "going crazy," "losing control," "making mistakes," and "being punished" to "losing one's sense of self." However, most of my audience members also say that they do deeply crave a stronger connection with the Divine. This ambiguity effectively puts one foot on the brake pedal and one foot on the gas.

The unbearable pain from the heresy and witch slayings from 1300 to 1700, in which people who were spiritually "different" were put to death in the most heinous ways, still permeates our world. The Inquisition is a part of what Carl Jung called our "collective unconscious," and its devastating aftereffects have made some of us fear communicating with Heaven. Somewhere, within our minds, we remember being put to death for talking to angels.

Fortunately, the archangels and angels can heal these deep-seated fears, and thereby effectively unclog our spiritual sense of hearing, vision, and touch. They can free us from the ancient shackles that bind us in dark emotional dungeons, isolated from Heaven's loving call.

So, in the final section of this book, I've described some methods that can help you become more aware of your guardian angels' messages. As you read the angel messages in this book, you'll receive personalized messages from your *own* angels, and this communication will come through your feelings, thoughts, visions, or an inner voice. I urge you to take note of these personal messages, as they may contain the answers to your prayers.

I've always found that when I ask Heaven to help me, my prayers are answered. The answers don't always come to me like a lightning bolt or a loud voice from above. They usually appear more subtly—through inner senses; synchronicities; and strong, repetitive ideas. In the final chapters of this book, I discuss ways to determine whether you're really hearing Heaven's voice or not.

As we release the fears that block us from receiving and recognizing messages from our angels, we become more aware of the presence of love in our lives. Our hearts expand, and we become kinder and more com-passionate. We find greater meaning in life—a sense of direction and purpose.

The angels are with us as a gift from our Creator, and their aim is to establish peace on Earth, one person at a time. Working wing-in-hand with the angels, I believe that this goal *is* possible.

Introduction

by the Angelic Realm

You who seek answers will find them, as you consult your own angels while reading our words. We are those who are among you night and day, and who steadfastly refuse to see you in any way except by the holy light that burns within you. We are your unwavering friends, your ceaseless companions, and your continuous comrades. We, your angels, hover slightly above you only because we are unmired by Earth's soiled viewpoints about existence. Where you may see hopelessness, we always see hope. Where you may see ravaged scars, we always see health. Where you may experience prolonged agony, we always see the way out of pain.

We are your champions, your allies, your greatest admirers, and your dynamic coaches. We are your angels, and we shall love you throughout eternity. How could it be any other way? Without love, we would all cease to be. And since God's handiwork can never be erased or confiscated, love can never diminish. And love, you understand, is who you are. Your love is unwavering, like a steady flame, undaunted by the wind around it. Your love *is* happiness, *is* peace, *is* immortality, and *is* abundantly cared for.

You need not travel an arduous or treacherous journey to arrive home. You are already there. All of your needs are provided for, as we seek to help you climb the wall to escape the products of your own nightmares. We are in the self-made prison with you, urging you to choose escape. We help you traverse the walls, and safely transition to your realization of complete freedom—freedom from all worries, cares, and concerns . . . if you so choose.

For some among you would choose otherwise, believing that pain is inescapable. Or rather, that pain is a necessary component to this process that you call "life." Yet, we are here to testify otherwise. That other choices can and do exist, and you can simply erase the bad effects of other choices with your holy and mighty will. You, who are all-powerful, have this "escape clause" scripted within your very being.

Pain is one means to growth—yes, this is quite true. Yet, you have heard us angels counsel you on other variables at your disposal. For, ultimately, you are already "grown." You are the product of Divine creation, and as such, you are already completely formed in all ways. Your learning, then, is illusory. "Learning" is actually "unlearning," where you forget your ego-established ideas. You lessen the pull of the ego, and gradually replace its lens with that of your higher self. You grow by unlearning the ego's perilous thought system and recalling your Divine origin. Do you need pain to unlearn this, when pain is the ego's primary creation? Surely, you witness the circular reasoning that the ego uses to keep you fascinated with its growth loop. Nothing can permeate the ego's defense system, and your escape is merely to step away and remember love.

Divine love always has been, and always will be, the answer that you seek. No matter what form it comes packaged in, this fact is inescapable. Nor would you want to escape love's holiness, and its pristine appreciation for who you truly are. Here is the all-encompassing womb you have been seeking. Here is the holy kiss and embrace that you crave. Here is the soulmate of all soulmates: It is your own Divine love.

Learn then, through unlearning mistakes in consciousness that formerly told you about mistakes in your creation. Grow, also, through recalling your holy origin. Learn and grow gently, through unlearning pain and remembering love, and you shall unravel the entanglements that once snared you. Let not one more moment slip by without an awareness of the pulsating love that beats steadily within you like a drum's rhythms, perfectly synchronized with God's outpouring of joy.

You are God's greatest triumph, and as you revel in your recovered awareness of this plain fact, allow us angels to slip off all layers of painful soot collected through your travels. Allow us to dust away sad memories and unpleasant journeys. Your new aspects await you, as graceful as a ballerina, as gentle as a lily pad, and as secure as any fortress. You are home, you are safe, and you are loved. Now and always.

PART 1

~~

Messages from
Your Angels

ꞓꞓ Breath ꞓꞓ

A h yes, your relationship to oxygen. The very breath that you take at this moment is fueled by a desire to continue upon this path that you have started. Some may say that breath is an automatic instinct, but from our perspective, it is a behavior that you engage in, as confirmation of your desire to stay upon the earth.

Each breath contains information within its molecular structure. We are in charge of this exchange of information. For, as you continue with your stay upon Earth, you need sustenance and assistance. We imbue each molecule of precious oxygen with guidance and instructions. It is our chief means of staying in touch with you, and within you.

Your breath is tantamount to a continuous meeting between us angels, your higher consciousness, and your Earthly self. It is a roundtable discussion, in which your next move is planned, and then the next. All of this is based upon your intentions, you see. With your outbreath, we are able to extract from you that which you no longer desire. And with your inbreath, we imbue positive direction that holds you up in the face of apparent discourse.

The stronger your desire, the stronger your breath. That is why during moments of strong desire, your breath deepens, and during moments when you feel helpless, your breath is shallow. Anytime you desire to create strong and rapid movement in your life, simply deepen your breath while perceiving your desire. You can achieve this through physical exertion, or simply through breath combined with meditation.

This formula may seem quite simple, yet we assure you that it is a powerful one that is instilled deep within your subconscious mind. So often we see you weary and in need of our help. You call upon us, yet our effectiveness is hampered by your slow and shallow breath. Right now, draw upon a deep and elongated breath while you call upon us for assistance. You shall feel our presence as you inhale.

When we encourage you to exercise, we do so partly to encourage this deeper form of breath. We know that you have noticed how many of your questions and troubles are answered at the conclusion of your exercise activities. That is because we are deeply transmitting to you along your exercise route. We are instilling you with comfort, guidance, and new perspectives on the situations at hand.

Awareness of your breath is essential for you at this time. Breathe deeply into your belly, and enjoy the sensation of filling your lungs. Take care *where* you breathe as well. We often engender a decision to move to a new locale where a higher grade of oxygen can be found. The higher the percentage of oxygen within each breath, the greater our degree of transmission to you. This is why it is more difficult to hear us when you block your body from receiving oxygen through such activities as smoking, drinking alcohol or carbonated drinks, and breathing fumes and polluted air.

That is one more reason why we ask you to join with us in dispensing toxic soot from your air, as it diminishes our abilities to freely communicate with you and all beings. We shall discuss this topic further, for it deserves great attention all its own. For now, then, dear child of God, establish your foothold firmly by concentrating upon deepening and strengthening your breath. Then, we shall see what information is in store for you—information that can free you in so many ways!

⊱ Child Conception ⊰

The holy union of two souls, calling together a third soul of a child, is among the most sacred rituals upon the earth. On the deepest level, this process is conscious, with every party performing their function perfectly. How could it be otherwise in God's perfect plan? Yet, you can uncover this wondrous process and bring it to conscious awareness in order to enhance your enjoyment and awareness.

Conscious child conception is akin to an awareness of other sacred activities such as manifestation, healing, and lucid dreaming. Yet, there is danger inherent in being aware of any of these processes. That danger lies in establishing an ego foothold in the process. In other words, when your ego takes the role of leadership during sacred moments, the process then becomes one where the ego seeks to establish its power, strength, and reality.

The ego urges you to accomplish, while the soul merely asks you to enjoy the process. With the ego in charge, there is a sense of strain, as if you are trying to *make* something occur. The soul's very purpose is antithetical to the ego's in this respect. For, the soul merely enjoys the process as it occurs. It does not seek to glorify itself, as the ego does.

That is why so many couples who deeply desire a child go childless. They have allowed strain and worry to intermingle with the sacred process of child conception, instead of practicing joyful awareness. Nowhere is a situation more appropriately geared toward "letting go and letting God" than with child conception. With great surrender, you erase pressures that thwart your very goal to bear a child! With gratitude shared during the time of coupling, you call upon the highest sense of your forthcoming child's soul.

The child's soul [we'll call it "she" for ease of reference] is reluctant to come forward when she senses strain within her parents' minds. She seeks a time of peace and joy, for optimum manifestation of the embryo occurs within these charitable conditions. Why would a child elect to have her body conceived under arduous conditions, when she wants the best possible chance for it to thrive and grow strong? It is better that she wait until a moment of coupling that is engendered with sweet love. At that time, her mother's womb is warm and inviting, and the child gladly leaps into the process of her body's conception.

Only a child involved in the drama of pain and suffering would desire to conceive when her parents are straining for conception. Such a child will have many opportunities throughout life to notice and heal this pattern. So much better for all concerned, to begin life on a peaceful note.

When coupling with the intention of childbearing, then, wise parents will take measures to fill their heart-spaces with great joy and gratitude. They will revel in the wisdom of their child's decision to come forward at the optimum moment. Rather than force the situation, they will surrender into each others' arms with gratitude at the perfection of each moment. Wrapped in affection, the womb pulsates with love that is irresistible to the forthcoming child. With the attraction and pull in place, the child's conception is inevitable.

❧ Departed Loved Ones ❧

The sorrow that you feel as you consider your loved ones who have departed from the Earth level is akin to sorrow related to any change that you cling to, wishing that it were not so. You underscore your sorrow by denying your knowledge that this transition is both necessary and a blessing. You curse the very formula of birth and death, and desire a different scenario that cannot be.

Your loved ones are never out of reach—not now or ever—for souls are constantly in communication with one another, especially when familial love is involved. This eternal connection keeps you close to one another through all of existence. How could it be otherwise, when your very soul tells you that this is so? Your soul, incapable of lies or capriciousness, knows that all of your loved ones—on the Earth plane and beyond—are at this very moment enshrouded in God's ecstatic joy. You, who seem joyless, are merely shedding God's warm blanket in favor of the chill of seeming apart, alone, and friendless. There is a comfort in your sorrow, and yet we beseech you to reconsider this decision.

For true joining with your loved ones comes from connecting with them in the inner glow of God's eternal joy. When you transmit joy to your loved ones, there is a bond so deep that it runs without words. Everyone concerned is aware of it, on a conscious level or otherwise. This connection is the solace that you seek, Dear One.

In a state of sorrow, you are assured of only one condition, and that is more sorrow. We cannot help you when you have decided upon this state of being. We merely stand by, ready to assist you the moment that you are satiated with this condition.

The leap from sorrow to joy may seem too large to traverse, and that is why you need our assistance. Within the space of no-time, we can help your heart to truly connect with your loved ones in the place where they currently reside. Their souls, like yours, live eternally in union with God and all others. And that place, as best we can capture in human terms, is called "joy."

When you ask how your departed loved ones are faring, you are inquiring as to whether they are happy or whether they are suffering. You also ask this question because you fear that you may have disappointed your loved one in some fashion. You have worry and guilt surrounding your sorrow, and no one to turn to for relief of these conditions. Yet, we can help you to know that your loved one, like yourself, is enshrouded in joy.

To do so, we will need some moments alone with you, however. We will need you to seal a space with conditions of quiet and peace. When you have fixed your Earthly space, call upon us angels to bring your awareness together with your loved one. We will ask you to breathe deeply, to concentrate upon your heart-space, and to fill it with great joy. We will ask you to recall joyful moments that you shared with your loved one. And as your heart warms and swells, you will feel the connection deepen with your loved one. You meet in that place of joy within your merged heart-space.

And always, even without our assistance, you can meet your loved one in this sacred place of joy. Do not concern yourself that you are violating any precepts or conditions with this meeting, for your souls are forever merged in joy, despite outward appearances to the contrary. When you travel with conscious awareness to this holy meeting ground, you go with the blessings of Heaven upon you. You return revived and reassured, and your doubts melt away like ice upon a summer sidewalk. Joy is all there is. The rest is a preoccupation of the ego, unworthy of your holy mind.

Always, your loved ones have loved you. Always, your loved ones revel in this eternal love for you. No room for anger, suffering, or pain of any kind, your loved ones implore you to dedicate your life and your schedule toward the embodiment of peace.

⚆ Emotional Healing ⚆

Many of you have suffered the wounds of childhood and early life, which seem to follow you forward in time. This is only because you have not taken the time to pause and understand them, and you worry about them. By holding questions about your earlier situations, life seeks to answer you with situations that potentially offer you answers. You may call this a "pattern of abuse," but life, being neutral, is merely answering your inquiries, such as "Why me?"

You call forth similar situations by focusing on these conditions in your thoughts and awareness. Surely, you must understand the truth of what we speak. As you realize this truth, your next response is that you are done with this repetition. And instead of asking more questions about your past, you seek to create a present time filled with joy and peace. We are awaiting this decision on your behalf. We surely cannot foist it upon you until such time as you request it.

So many times you have expected the worst, and life has delivered your expectations flawlessly. Do you see, within these examples, the depth of your power in directing your scenes? Emotional healing does not mean dwelling upon the wound; it means looking at the world through unwounded eyes. Our words are not callous, for we have great compassion for your suffering. We simply seek to unravel you from the grip of ancient wounds so that you can experience the freedom that you seek.

So many stay mired in past situations, hunting for reasons or even for revenge. Rise above such temptations, Holy One, and commit to a new way of living. Your true and inner self is unscarred, unwounded, and fully confident in living a peaceful life so that all may benefit. *Healing*, then, means *revealing* that which is already enacted. What you set your heart upon must come about. If you seek validation of your woundedness, you shall surely find that. Yet, if you seek, instead, confirmation of your inner strength and power, that shall you find as well.

Heal, then, through your commitment to revealing the holy essence that you are in truth. Heal your emotional scars by casting them aside, while delving headfirst into a new direction—one of superb inner strength, one that translates into giving you opportunities to help others through their adversities, and one that does justice to your holy self.

ᵔᵊᵔ Exercise ᵔᵊᵔ

So many times we have attempted to encourage you to take better care of your physical body, and so often, our attempts have been thwarted. You travel this way and that in an exhausting measure to ensure that your body remains untoned and static. The exertion of exercise pales before the intensity with which you resist this endeavor. We could motivate you a thousand times over, and yet be flattened by your decision to wait, wait, wait.

Wait no longer, Holy Child, for you are given a body as a timeline device, to be used in holy service of the shining Light. Your joyfulness is of a high dimension, yet this Earthly tool called a "body" must be maintained if you are to see the mission through. Ignoring this instrument is bound to leave it gasping for oxygen and movement, both essential to its sustenance.

The body was engendered with movement, and was created through this very process during your Earthly parents' coupling. It moved inside your mother's womb, and it craves movement throughout its lifetime. Yet, your oversoul controls the amount and duration that the body is allowed to move. Your oversoul can restrict the body's movements with its internal commands. And for this, the body shrivels and suffers.

Movement is essential food for the body, Beloved Ones. This message is eternal, yet even more essential at this point in time. No matter what course or form this movement takes on, it is movement for movement's sake that your body requires.

Use any excuse for movement, then. Climb a staircase, take a walk, or march in place. The movement is essential to the progress of the Light, moving to cover all human consciousness and awareness.

ꝏꝰ Father ꝰꝏ

So many of you have poor relationships with your physical fathers, resulting in and stemming from a poor relationship with your own male side. For you see, despite your body's genetic coding, your maleness is inherent within the human condition, just as your femaleness coexists as well. At this time in human history, the femaleness is arching upward, making her presence known. A danger of imbalance exists if you allow the female to outweigh the male, for neither is superior, and both are necessary for balance and fruition.

Your physical father's own upbringing was very difficult because of this transitory time, where human drama moved away from honoring the male and spat upon him in many ways. This transition horrified your father, who had no way to predict or understand this turmoil within human civilization. All that he knew was that his maleness was rejected and regarded as something foreign and unacceptable. And yet, his maleness made up much of his identity. Without any resource to turn to, your father turned on his very own self with a form of self-hatred. He was disheartened, and his heart was broken.

He cast himself away from you and your siblings in a veiled attempt to save you from him. Feeling valueless, he continued his charade of providing sustenance for the family, all the while feeling valueless himself. He hadn't a clue of his true value, both as a holy child of God and as a protector of the family in so many ways. You, my child, suffered at your father's hands because of his lack of awareness. He knew not love, nor could he show it sufficiently. Thus, you reorganized your life in a valiant effort to show your superiority so that your father's pride could shine upon you. Yet, you always shrank away from facing your worst-feared truth: that your father could not love you, and could not provide for you in the way that you had hoped.

So you looked for his approval in many ways, finally falling exhausted and weary from the efforts, and always falling short of your prize. Will you now turn away from attempts to capture the uncapturable,

Beloved One? Will you now see that your father prized you as much as he was capable, but that he was incapable of expressing this in words? It was because of the nature of the societal transition that devalued men, Dear One. This plummet in male self-worth made him regard himself as having no sure foothold in your life, no impact that had any value. So, instead, he cast off child care to your mother, who was also unsure of her place in your life. You, seeking a solid foundation of approval, warmth, and love, assumed that you had erred, lest you would surely gain your parents' steady love and approval. *What have I done wrong to have pushed them away?* you wondered.

Beloved Child of God, you have done nothing wrong, and we assure you that you are wholly lovable—then, now, and always. Forgive your father. Forgive yourself. Move on into eternity with a gladdened heart, knowing that your true Father and Mother in Heaven will love and comfort you always.

～ Forgiveness ～

Forgiveness ends suffering that stems from harboring rage toward oneself or others. It lets the air out of the balloon of holding one's breath, filled with anger. When you decide that a wrong has occurred—regardless of the perpetrator—you place that situation into a prison cell and hold it captive in your consciousness. The perception of "evil" that you harbor within yourself is akin to swallowing a foreign virus that subsequently attacks your physical self. It is impossible to perceive evil and harbor it in consciousness and not have it negatively impact you.

Forgiveness frees these unwanted tenants from your system, freeing you to heal on many dimensions. When we speak of forgiveness, though, we see certain efforts in this direction falling short of their mark. Forgiveness with judgment is ineffective. To be free is to release the judgment of wrongdoing entirely. Give the situation to God and the angels, and know that we will effectively guide the situation—and all involved. In that way, you will not need to be the captor or the judge of the situation or people, whether they be "perpetrators" or "victims."

You are given the power to heal, a power so lovely that if you cast your eyes before it, you would fall to your knees in awe of the Creator's great gift to you! Your willingness to utilize your power in the name of healing is a chief incentive for you to allow forgiveness to reign. You are not forgiving because of some prescript, but because you *can* forgive. You are not forgiving to gain or to lose something, but because you *can* forgive. Your power is so great that you have the ability to forgive all . . . for all.

Forgive yourself, Darling Child of God, for your harsh judgments of your reality! You have selected instances of your life, and judged them strongly with malice. Yet, is this a way to heal yourself or others? Does such self-judgment remove your consciousness from the Light? For the only judgment worthy of you is this: In each situation, ask whether each thought, each word, and each deed creates a greater or a lesser awareness of love.

ꙮ Freedom ꙮ

What we see around you at this time is a great cost being paid for the price of freedom. You forsake freedom a great deal of the time, and then you begin to crave it. At that point, you will do anything and pay anything to regain the freedom. Yet the freedom is yours for the taking at any time. Renegotiate your new definition of freedom with yourself.

You have, in may ways, painted yourself into a corner by collecting debts resulting from amassing items that you believe will give you freedom. Do you not see the irony of this circular situation? When you purchase items or experiences to lift yourself from a feeling of slavehood, then you have created an additional barrier for yourself. Escape totally from the barriers that confine you, Dear One! You do not need to be captured or controlled, for your will has the same roving freedom of your Creator and cannot be contained.

Your restrictions come first from the belief that you must work for your freedom. Do you not see the irony in this belief? Work can breed the very slavedom from which you seek to escape! Think carefully before signing an employment contract of any form. We see far too many of you exchanging your precious hour for a meager salary upon which you can barely subsist. Many of you, too, become your own captors through self-servitude, in what you call "self-employment."

Do you not see that a simpler answer awaits you just below the surface? It is called "self-emancipation." It comes from giving yourself healthy doses of freedom through the process of simplification, a reduction of expenditures, and a lightening of your load-of-debt ratio.

When you incur debt, you become beholden to the future, which casts you in the shadow of time servitude. This is the very cycle of which we speak: You take on a job that incurs your ire or wrath. You purchase items beyond your means to help you cope with your situation. You then must stay with this path in order to meet your financial obligations. This is the route to utter misery, meaninglessness, and time-wasting preoccupations. Do you not see that much greater vistas await you now?

You can fly as free as the birds, without constraint or time restrictions. This you can achieve right now! The only restriction is the limitation in your beliefs that prevent you from breaking free from self-made imprisonment.

Think for a moment about what is resting heavily upon your soul: situations, relationships, obligations, and so on. Then picture what a different scenario might be like. How would you feel to be free from the imprisonment? Do not worry about *how* this could occur. Just enjoy the freedom on a mental or emotional level. Do not question it, wonder about it, or worry about its fathomability. Just hold it in your belly and heart, and imagine that it is so. Do not advertise your new conquest openly as of yet. Keep it to yourself. And as it comes to you on the waking plane, watch for any tendencies to bypass your new freedom with additional slavedom.

You truly hold the key to your prisons through imagining the cell door being opened wide. Can you allow yourself to imagine this freedom, Beloved One? We pray that it is so, because as you open your prison doors widely, so do you allow others the escape they desire.

⊷ Gratitude ⊶

Gratitude is the key to living a consistent life. No more must you deal with altitudes and plummets when you concern yourself solely with gratitude. Yet, let us discuss this term, for it is often misunderstood. Gratitude is often mistaken for humility, in which you grovel with thanksgiving for your supplies. This is surely one form that gratitude must take from time to time, yet the most surefooted way to place yourself on the path of a harmonious existence is through gratitude that is more heart-centered.

What we mean is this: In addition to showing gratitude to others, place emphasis on showing gratitude to yourself. Your heart-center glows brightly with love as you praise it for its very existence. Praise your inner glow so that its embers may burn even brighter. Give thanks to your in-soul (what you refer to as your "higher self") for providing you with relief and solace. Give thanks to God within you so that you may extend this love ever outward in a widening circle of gladness.

Do you see the difference, then, between this heart-centered approach to gratitude? In one instance, you give thanks outwardly for what has been given to you from outside of yourself. Yet, this is but a manifestation of the glow within. Do not see God as separated from your inner embers. Know that He created, and continues to stoke, this original flame. Your light can never be extinguished, as we have repeatedly reminded you. Your only task is to ensure that its glow burns ever more brightly, allowing it to shine for all to see.

When you give gratitude to your inward light, you fan its flames with your praise. It warms to your gratitude, which encourages it to grow larger and brighter. As your light grows larger, so will your outward manifestations increase as well. You will have much to feel grateful toward with this process—we assure you!

Do not worry, dear children, that this is a selfish style of praise and gratitude. Always remember that the Source of your soul's light is God, Whom you praise. Always remember that God's Divine Light burns within you now and always. And as you fill this Light with praise, it is as if you have filled your inner room with a thousand candles' glow.

Notice carefully the outward manifestations that come to you as you engage in this process. The first will be joy, followed by a sense of security and peacefulness. Surely you will agree that these are valuable commodities! Then, as you continue to bless your heart-center, you will witness a new style of living for yourself. You may find a wealth of emotions that are too strong for you to experience as yet. When this occurs, seek shelter in peaceful locations with loved ones or us angels. You will feel strong compassion from us, and discover interesting new ventures. You will receive many opportunities and goods that may help you along the way.

Your inner light has another benefit as well, because it can extinguish the dross from each experience that comes to you. When your outward manifestations seem to counteract your joy, you can picture the mistakes, the pain, or the troubles all burning in the incinerator within your mighty flame. You have this powerful heart-center as God's gift during your Earthly path . . . to guide you, to manifest for you, and to clear you of any wreckage along the way.

❧ Guilt ❧

When guilt weighs upon your holy mind, Heaven weeps on your behalf for your errant decision to dethrone yourself. Do you not know the eternal innocence of each of God's holy children? The instant that you choose to see "badness" within yourself, a cyclical process happens. First, your in-soul, what you often refer to as your "higher self," shrivels at the thought that it has made a mistake, created displeasure in you, and incurred your wrath. When your soul shrivels, your light literally shrinks in size. This reduces your power and effectiveness in the world—not in reality, but as the world perceives you. Those with ego mind-sets may viciously attack you, as a wild animal preys upon the sick and weary.

Your guilt is a doomsday sentence that puts your body at great discomfort and even danger. For guilt always expects a reprimand, and it does not rest until this punishment occurs. The guilt-ridden soul will seek out pain to appease and atone for its mistake. This creates a negative mind-set, complete with negative intentions. Your mind expects punishment, so you begin scanning the horizon, expecting to *find* the punishment. And you already know that whatever you seek, you will find. It is also true, though, that you will create and attract whatever you seek. A guilt-ridden mind will create and attract one negative situation after another. The in-soul will decide that you deserve this pain, and it will continue to attract more in an endless fashion.

So, do you see the deep and inherent danger of holding on to guilt? You have not made any mistakes in truth, and you certainly do not deserve punishment of any sort. There are no Earthly mistakes that you could possibly make that could undo God's eternal handiwork. He created you perfectly, and you do not have the power to make yourself imperfect—no matter how hard you may try!

Your Earthly mistakes may be ghastly and may have caused much pain, but God holds you guiltless still. In His eyes, you and your siblings are the most beautiful beings in the universe. God and the angels look past your Earthly mistakes and see within you your eternal flame of Divine love. We know that this is the only vantage point that will help you. As we gaze upon your inner God-self, we increase the size and brightness of your light. This larger light in your in-soul is the only remedy for your mistakes, Dear One. Only a larger light will help to lead you away from negative situations. Only by loving that light that God placed inside of you can you find the lantern to illuminate your path toward happiness.

Say to yourself, "I am love. I am love and light." See it and know this to be true. And whenever you are tempted to seek pain or punishment, remember our words.

❧ Healing ❧

Everything is already healed, except in the dream of illness. When you focus upon the problem at hand, you enlarge it in every sense of the word. Do not allow this to offend you, since you expect some reward for your compassion for worldly and personal problems. The compassion that you offer has not been lost or overlooked. It has simply been restyled. What is called for is a new brand of compassion, Beloved One. This entails looking past the illusion that you call the problem in the first place. Perhaps you know that it is the first law of metaphysics that whatever you focus upon grows and enlarges. Why, then, do you imagine that your negative compassion for problems will help them to heal?

Why not, instead, focus upon *positive* compassion, in which you imagine that the situation is already healed and curtailed? Do not worry that this could usurp the will of God or others. This positive compassion merely calls into being that which has already been Divinely created: perfection. This perfection is instilled inside the very life-force that you breathe. And by focusing upon solutions, instead of problems, you incur the life-force in its natural direction.

Simply see the situation, no matter its topic or appearance, as already resolved. Give thanks that it is so. And accept this healed situation into your heart, without regard for matter or logic. Even an ounce of belief will go far along the pathway to revealing the healed underpinnings of every seeming problem.

This is true for any body, large as the earth's very ocean or atmosphere, or the tiniest body of a microscopic organism or puny animal. Hold the truth in consciousness that sickness cannot exist in the face of love, and you will reveal the greatest reality of them all.

⁓ Healing the Body ⁓

Healing stems from your decision to share the love that is yours to begin with. To share this love is a commitment and a decision. When you commit and decide for this purpose, you naturally create new avenues to do so. You also eradicate anything that stands in the way. When sharing love is your utmost priority, you will take action to ensure its fruition.

You will heal your body, your life, and your mind because you must have these tools to share love with others. Do it for your purpose, and you will find that your healing rushes to meet you! Healing, as we have previously explained, is more accurately referred to as "revealing," as this is the truth behind this principle.

Healing, when properly understood, merely means casting a firm decision in the direction of your higher self's priorities. When you bow to the ego's whims and dictates, you allow fear to stand in the way. Your self-consciousness makes you weak, yet how could God's creation be anything but strong? God did not create weakness—you did—with your decision that weakness gave you more than strength did. And you can rethink this decision in order to experience differing results.

Revealing is best approached with a heart that is open to gratitude for God's power. You already have all that you need, and you are merely reminded of this essential truth. Your access to health is eternally available, and you need merely claim this because you desire more available time and energy for your holy purpose. Your clear and unwavering decision for health cannot be obstructed, Holy Child of God. Your unquestionable power rests upon your decision, your intention, and your commitment. There is no force opposed to your own. In this, your will and God's will co-exist in perfect harmony.

~ Job Burnout ~

Many of you are turning to Heaven for help in escaping jobs that you can no longer withstand. This is an appropriate way in which to work with your angels, for we are freedom show-ers. We know that you feel constricted at your workplace, and that you seek a means to follow the natural rhythms of your being. You dream of self-employment, or a way to magically transform your career into one with greater autonomy and meaning. You have outgrown your present situation, yet you feel that you cannot afford to let this one go.

In this bind of financial insecurity, with so many pressures upon you, you run out of time, energy, and inspiration that could fuel your new venture. You remain trapped, and your soul collapses in exhaustion, unable to escape this daily grind. Your boredom is coupled with too much time spent indoors, a volatile combination to be sure. All of this is unnatural behavior, and we are happy that you and others are increasingly becoming more natural, or at least are in the direction of that attempt.

Becoming natural means that you trust and follow the guidance of your heart. Being unnatural means refusing to follow love's ways, and placing barriers around your soul. But you cannot put love into a box, shut it away, and expect it to shine! You, who have so much to add to this world, only leave victimhood as your legacy when you betray yourself in this way. Are you teaching your children empowerment or victimhood with your approach to your job?

If there is something that you desire, you have the means to attain it. You only need to be clear about what it is that you want, pray for guidance, and then motivate yourself to take the necessary steps that are guided. To deny this avenue of "escape" is to deny your Godliness. You are not victim to any illusion of false security unless complacency keeps you there. We will give you a gentle and gradual plan of escape, or help you to heal an intolerable situation so that there are blessings for all concerned.

There is no need for anger, impulsiveness, or frustration. You are given the key to unlock your prison immediately, and you only need fearlessly place your key into the lock to escape. The power is given to you at any given moment. Myriad solutions await your beck and call, if only you will set your mind on the dial of "solutions" instead of "problems." Have hope for the betterment of yourself and your family. Hopelessness breeds only dead ends. God cannot thrust solutions onto you, but He does await your prayers for guidance to help you reach your own happy endings.

You have much to offer the world, Dear One! You are multitalented beyond your scope of understanding. Some of your talents require polishing, patience, and training. Yet, they are your talents, nonetheless. They are also the root of your passions, and they form the basis of the path of your life's purpose. You have the power, with your focused intention, to create a career that is rooted in your life's purpose. There is no happier career than this!

Our prayer is that you will know that you are qualified, and that you deserve, this career of passion and purpose. Our prayer is that you will call upon us for guidance, and that you will surely follow it as it is given. Our prayer is that you will trust.

~∾ Life Path ∾~

Every moment of your life is an opportunity to serve, and thus, is an opportunity to be joyful. Your service can be to the living planet or any of its inhabitants. One of the reasons why we angels are so joyful is that we are continuously focused upon giving service. This does not mean being a martyr or a doormat—oh, no, far from it! Such negative connotations occur when giving comes from a sense of guilt or obligation. That type of giving helps neither the giver nor the recipient. But giving from a place of abundance, where you know that you have much to give, brings joy to all. We are not focusing the word *giving* on material giving necessarily. The giving and service can be as simple as feeding a hungry animal or smiling at a lonely child. And by so doing, you are *given to* in abundance.

Search the horizon for opportunities to serve, and they will present themselves readily to you. You have angels assisting you in your service work, so approach your giving with your Heavenly teammates, and do not hesitate to call upon us to support your service work. You have so much to give, yet you do not see it if you do not give willingly and freely. This crumbles your "self-esteem," because it is only through giving that you fall in love with your life and your God. The love of God reflects upon the love of your higher self, which elevates your opinion of yourself—not in a lofty or arrogant manner, but in a way that recognizes love as itself.

Your life path, then, is one hinging upon discovering your true nature through service and giving. Hesitate not in giving, awaiting some faraway perfect time and opportunity to give. Seek for it now, and discover its awaiting presence, lying patiently for your discovery. The more that you give, the more you shall truly have. And yet, this is merely a trite saying without action behind its words. Experiment with giving, and discover the results firsthand. In that way, you shall know the truth of our words: You are a giver, and you are amply given to.

Be open to receiving the good that comes to you each day. Resist not the plethora of plentitude that God bestows upon you. Through gracious receiving, you know that you are amply blessed. This knowledge gives you the confidence to keep on giving . . . through joyful service.

~&~ Lightwork ~&~

Because there is no time to be wasted (since there is no time to begin with, and in the world that measures time, it is *now* with which we are concerned), we ask that you be open to our assignments. We assure you that they are not beyond the scope of your interests or abilities, and many of these assignments will be quite pleasant. Certainly, they will bring you closer to that place which you may refer to as "home."

You may worry about how you can succeed in this aspect, but that is a projection of your old standards of succeeding, using such templates as grades, raises, and promotions. In lightwork, such terms are meaningless. Whether you are progressing financially is unrelated to your remembrance work spiritually. One is involved in collecting, and the other is involved in unveiling. Remember that you have both types of riches available to you instantly—the moment that you untangle yourself from low or lofty projections and simply arrive in a place of universal love.

When you place your faith in the Creator within and above, as the Source for which you have been waiting, you can move ahead easily with your lightwork. You do not have to worry or wait for a moment to escape prior to effecting your teaching and healing ministry. No, these efforts are best projected in the present, rather than in the future.

There is nothing and no one preventing you from enjoying your life purpose. You are an entirely free agent, no matter what appearances may seem to prevail. At every moment, there is a person or situation who could benefit from your application of Divine light, love, and vision. Focus upon finding these people and situations, rather than upon any seeming blocks. Always remember that you are the director of the movie script in which you find yourself. A positive intention will bring you your desired outcomes, and a pessimistic intention will always block you.

Do you know that you deserve to be immersed in positive outcomes? These are not rewards, so much as they are options that are available to all. The path to learning can come in many forms, and one form is not more favored by God. All the forms—uplifting, depressing, and everything in between—are among the freewill choices given to you by your Creator, Who simply hopes that you will choose the best for yourself and those among you.

~ Manifestation ~

Manifest means to "invest" or to "store." The term is rightly used in these two definitions, for manifestation is rooted where you invest or store your focus and intention. We see many people investigating the topic of manifestation through this book or that course, yet the principle is plainly available for all to see. What you set your sights upon, with clear intention, is what you steer toward. It is what you draw into your life. This principle cannot be forced, because pressure comes from a sense of anxiety that undermines your efforts. Rather, an ease or comfort, as you steer toward your desire, will bring it rapidly to your side.

Many of you ask, "What if this is not God's will?" and we ask you in return, "Are you making this inquiry with the assumption that God is a part of you who asks?" For what will could there be but God's will? Yes, the lesser ego choices can steer you toward objectives, but you will always correct them, as your overriding intention will always be in the direction of joy. Nowhere could the ego's intentions bring about joy of any sort. Always, God's intentions are rooted in joy.

So God's will, which resides within you always, directs you toward joy by reminding you that you are already immersed in this joy. The pleasure that you seek is attained the instant that you allow yourself to enjoy the gift that is already given to you. You structure your time by seeking outward manifestations of this inward joy. There are no "wrong" manifestations, simply intentions that immerse you in joy, or intentions that remove your awareness of joy. The "object" of your intention cannot be wrong or apart from God's will, because God—and God's will— only know joy.

It is possible for you to know joyfulness in your heart, without interruption. This is an intention that is truly worthy of your devotion. No matter what the material or situational intention, approach them with the desire for joy. Know that your joy comes not in the future, tied in with your material or situational intention. Rather, your joy accompanies you now, and stays with you as you manifest your other desires. The power of this joy cannot be overemphasized. It lights the pathway of your manifestation process. It allows you greater access to the surefooted guidance that you seek.

Reveal the joy now by holding the intention: "My heart and mind are now filled with joy. I am a mighty reflection of God's happiness." Train your mind upon this desire, and feel the joy pulsate through your being. Fear not the happiness if it seems like an unfamiliar stranger. It is an angel, enveloping you in wings from within your heart-center. Joy keeps you strong and provides you access to creative wisdom. Its magical properties have no negative side effects, just the ability to place you on the smooth ride of consistent joy. It is possible to find joy, no matter what your outward circumstances appear to be. And as you find this joy, keep it close to your heart, and watch your negative outward circumstances fall away.

Reach inwardly and touch this truth without delay. Feel the essence of that which we speak, Dear One. Drink in the nectar that your heart-space offers you: the joy that you desire, that you deserve, that is yours, that is you. This is our loving prayer for you, our Beloved One.

Marriage

Marriage is a declaration that a couple wants to take their partnership to a higher level, to soar with the angels romantically, emotionally, physically, and spiritually. In that respect, it is symbolic of the desire for Heavenly union with love. It represents the desire for oneness, the merging with the Divine. Marriage seeks the changelessness of God, to create an oasis of peace in the midst of outer-worldly chaos.

So many hopes and dreams are pinned upon marriage that it sometimes falters under the crushing weight of dashed expectations. Yet, it is true that within the safe harbor of marriage, both partners can reach new levels of spiritual bliss that are unparalleled in less ordinary circumstances.

You who desire marriage, please remember that God's love is within you always. You who carry a torch for a marital partner are seeking for the light in another to merge with your own. Your hunger for marriage is beyond that of mere partnership. You seek to build the embers of your own Divine flame higher, bigger, and brighter. Through marriage, your two flames can join together to formulate one larger, brighter flame.

Yet, seek this experience first on your own. Seek to build your own immortal flame higher, bigger, and brighter as a means of expanding your self-knowledge of Divine love. This ensures that your light attracts to you a partnership worthy of your Divine heritage. And then, when you do merge your lights within marriage, you do so out of joy, not from empty neediness. You give your lights to each other in a holy dowry, building one another skyward so that your light shines from the heavens onto the earth's expanse.

And you, who are already in the midst of marriage, remember these words: that both bride and groom carry a torch within that seeks to fulfill its truth. Your merging of light, and thus your building of one another's light, is essential to the sanctity of your marriage. Seek always to see your partner's holy and Divine light and touch it to your own often, for as you kindle and tend to your partner's inner torch, you build the flame of your own, naturally. You and your partner soar Heavenward as you look for each other's holy flames. Your countenance only becomes heavy and dour when you cease this function and forget to look inward. An eternally happy marriage is built upon this covenant of flame-building, through building one another's spirit of joy. Create opportunities for these exchanges often, whether it be an exchange of kind words, shared deeds of mutual enjoyment, or a togetherness in life's purpose for the betterment of the world.

~ Mother ~

Your relationship with your mother is built upon the backbone of the Divine. It is essential to reach a deeper understanding of this relationship, for it is a springboard upon which so many other relationships falter or thrive. There is a hierarchy of relationships within your human life, and the cornerstone foundation for so many other relationships belongs to the parental category. Probably the greatest impact belongs to the "mothering" category, which may come as no surprise to you.

Your relationship with your mother is among the most important because it has a direct line to either your ego or your in-soul (what you call your "higher self"). You can reach the highest of heights with your mother, or the lowest of lows. Through these dizzying ups and downs, you always have the choice of which direction you next wish to pursue with your mother. Your decision is largely directed by what you expect. For expectations of "how" a relationship is, or "how" a person in your life behaves, is the steering mechanism that determines your next encounter.

A fixed decision that your mother is a certain way, then, almost always leads to a situation that confirms this decision. You therefore have the ability to switch directions in your relationship with her at your will. You, who have the power to move mountains, can most certainly manage this miracle!

For, your mother's impression is deeply imbedded within you. Your view of your mother largely creates your viewpoint of so many others, including yourself, your offspring, and your subsequent love relationships of each variety (friends, partners, and such).

When you switch your viewpoint of your mother to a loving one, then, the impact is wide-reaching and great. It may seem to take a great effort to view your mother in a more loving way, and this is where we angels may be of assistance. We can take your words of love and deliver them to your mother's heart wordlessly so that the impact of your loving thoughts is fully felt. Beloved One, this decision is yours, but we do assure you that such a decision would be worthwhile and beneficial to you and so many others!

≈ Music ≈

Music is essential to your lightwork at this juncture. Use the music to elevate your frequency as often as possible, since it bathes you in shimmering light that deflects away negativity. This airborne negativity, which could settle unknowingly into your consciousness, could create havoc, with your having little awareness of its origin. Music shields you from these free-floating patterns, creating more opportunities for you to be at peace.

Your choice of music is limitless, just as long as you utilize music in some fashion throughout your day and evening. The more you indulge in music, the greater your benefit, exponentially.

Some of you are able to ascertain the color bands that travel with the sound waves of music. Similar to the rainbow effects of high humidity, your music carries information encoded in visible colors. You, who are traveling at a high visual frequency, must learn to convey this information to others. You, who see the colors emitting from musical instruments and speakers, learn to trust the relevance of these visions.

These colors are emanations of the molecular structure of musical sounds. They bend light waves and bounce lesser molecules away from you, in the deflecting process that we described to you earlier. For, as you surround yourself with music, you wrap yourself in a blanket of these various colors. The musical molecules interact with the energy frequency patterns emanating from your body, in a dance with the hues that you call your "auric field." These electrical sparks are similar to the glowing colors that many of you see, which you have termed "angel lights" or "angel trails."

To be sure, there are colors of a higher vibrational frequency than others—what you would term your "cool shades." You choose music according to your moods, and this is partly to clothe yourself in various colors that suit you. The more lively music is often associated with the warmer colors of red, orange, and yellow, while the more soothing music is, not surprisingly, strongly associated with the violet, indigo, and green varieties. Use music in this way to enhance and elevate your emotions, as it brings about strong effects.

At times when you wish to reach inward at a deeper and more rapid pace, your choice in music would be different from when you desire a faster pace. We, who can easily see the effects of your musical choices, both in your energy state and in the colors that surround you, can become involved in helping you make conscious decisions about your music. Simply call upon us, and we will guide you without hesitation, without interference or control, and always with love surrounding our motivations.

❧ Pollution ❧

We are grateful that you are examining this situation concerning pollution, and that you are consulting with us for our opinion and direction upon this matter. For as much as it saddens you to face this topic, it is only through direct action that any measurable effect can come about. The concern for pollution comes from its effects upon all bodies upon the earth, in lowering their energy and morale, as the choking smog and toxic soil creates heaviness everywhere.

This is a case where Heaven and Earth must work in unison to make the shifts within matter, to avoid saturating the earth with toxins and pollutants that pierce through your body's defenses. You, who are working for the Light, must bring more physical light to the planet by allowing the sun's rays to reach your planet without filtration from soot in the air that you breathe.

In some areas of the universe, there is no need for oxygen because the bodies that inhabit the planet are built differently from your own. They are made of lighter, less dense materials, barely visible to human vision. Your own bodies would not be adaptable to such an environment, however, as you have lungs that inflate to propel your cardiovascular system with oxygen molecules. Without oxygen, your light would still shine, but dimmer still, and without the benefit of your body as a learning tool.

So, we seek to part the sooty darkness from the atmosphere surrounding this sacred planet, and let you breathe the fresh air that God intended for you. This air is a gift so sweet and soft that your first breath of it would cause you rapture. Yet, many have forgotten the feeling of ingesting sweet oxygen, and have adapted to air of a lesser quality.

There is pollution on your planet today because of your intention to provide goodness to yourselves through dense, material means. With the emphasis today that is upon the teaching or reteaching of the ancient sciences of manifestation, these old means should be eased out soon enough. When that occurs, your lesser dependence upon machinery will create relief upon the earth's soil and atmosphere. You will witness a cleansing like the earth has never before seen!

Yet, during this time of transition, with continued dependency upon machinery and increasing use of electrical telecommunications powers, we must advise you to seek another course for the manifestation of your cleaner environment. We see many of you taking means to use cleaner products within your household environments, and we assure you that such efforts are not minuscule by any means! Your intentions are charged with an energy that inspires and excites those around you, and you are thus a role model for caretaking of the environment. Never fear that your efforts go unnoticed or that they are wasted. Beloved One, you are deeply honored for your contributions, and every action of care for your planet is viewed as a highly significant act of great love.

You who are attempting to rid yourself of machinery and electrical dependency, your intentions are honored! You who are voluntarily changing your lifestyle to support the animals and farming to be free of noxious chemicals, you are honored! You who collect rubbish from the grounds of nature, you are honored! You, who invest in household goods that are less harsh than others, you are honored!

And together, we hold an eternal viewpoint of nature in her pristine glory. We do not saddle our thoughts about the planet with anger, or cloud our vision by seeing only the soot-filled air. No! We refuse to gaze at the mistakes, but peer beneath them to the beautiful truth that the planet's will for health is stronger than any environmental mistakes that could be temporarily inflicted. Join with us angels, then, in holding this elevated viewpoint of the clean and healthy planet body. See her body as healthy and healed, and you will soon discover the enormous power that such a viewpoint holds.

❧ Power Places ❧

Y^ou call them "vortexes," or "power spots," these geographical locations upon the planet where intense spiritual energies are said to be.
It is true that within these locations there are the remains of the energetic fingerprint of previous inhabitants. These special places are the
mark where previous ceremony infused the location with high amounts
of healing intentions. Prayer, rituals, chanting, and celebrations cleansed
the area beneath the participants' feet, leaving way for more energy to
become infused with the ground below.

These locations hold the memory of their previous inhabitants and
their sacred rituals. This effect was previously well known, and was used
to locate the place where a ceremony had been previously held. In some
cases, there was a lack of awareness of the building energy in the sacred
place, and the repetition of ceremony in this location was based upon
convenience, logic, and habit. The echoes of these ceremonies reverber-
ate from the surface to the deep recesses of each location, and the sensitive lightworkers among you can sense these reverberations. These are
the locations that you are referring to as "power places."

Yes, it is true that you can access the infused prayers within these
locations. Their healing effects would be most felt if you were to lie
down upon the ground where prayer ceremonies were held. Then, allow
those prayers to filter upward through your body, like life-giving x-rays
permeating your entire being. Before you exit this location, it is essential that you give back, by sending prayers into the ground. Seal the visitation by infusing the ground with your Divine thoughts and an intention of loving energy.

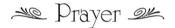

Prayer

Prayer is an internal form of meditation, which is essential to help one escape from fear. Allow prayer to bring you closer to the Light that is God, in whatever way the moment brings you. Do not seek to control your prayer, for it is as free-flowing as any conversation of great importance. Be in the moment with your prayer, and accept whatever thoughts or feelings accompany each moment. One moment you will be exuberant, the next sad or remorseful. Then, you will appeal to Heaven for help, followed by a quieter moment of reverence. Each moment spent in prayer is like a dime put into a bank account. We do not hold it there for you in trust. We let each prayer go along the wind, and still it belongs to you, with all the interest and benefits accruing daily. Accumulate your prayers and accept their assistance. Each one is your angel, helping you along.

We do not seek to assist your prayers, only to encourage you in their doing. Each morning is a fine time in which to begin your prayers. Ideally, before you awaken, you will engage in conversation with your Creator. And thus, as your head rests on the pillow and your eyes are sleepy still, you will awaken to the voice of your Beloved Creator. What a Heavenly way to enter into each day! And the power of such a positive entry will surely birth many days of happiness and miracles!

Then, throughout the day, reach up and inwardly connect with us through thoughtful prayer and meditation. These sacred glimpses into the Divine can refresh and replenish you immediately when you feel depleted. Simply cast your cares unto us, and let us cart them away as a janitor would carry away your garbage. You have no worries that you cannot thrust into our loving and awaiting arms, Dear One. Give them all away!

Prayer simply means "reconnection," and reconnection with the Divine is your lifeline to endless inspiration and vitality. Prayer has become, to some, entangled with rules or feelings of obligation. Yet, even obligatory prayer is highly powerful, and it gives added benefits to those who already shine. For, you see, prayer is like stopping at a fuel station to refortify yourself with gasoline, oil, and other necessities. You can engage in prayer during any moment of the day simply by holding in mind the intention to call home to Heaven. Hold the thought that you would like God's loving assistance, and it is done. Be assured that we are always available to assist you, and know that your prayers will never be denied.

Psychic Abilities

You have psychic abilities instilled in you because they are necessary for your holy mission. Not all are as aware as you are of the psychic transmissions that bombard all of humanity. Many must duck and run for cover from these transmissions lest their awareness of their imbalances become so acute that they are forced to make life changes. To weather the storm of a harsh life, some must turn off this faculty, and there is an understandable reluctance to reunite with their psychic side. This topic warrants some discussion, because all who can hear will do so soon enough. But that is not up to us; it is up to each individual to discover for him- or herself.

Once someone has had a psychic transmission, their life is altered beyond measure. They no longer look upon their surroundings in quite the same way, and their day-to-day tasks feel mundane and less meaningful. They seek to grow and share in more profound ways, thus creating chaos in their once orderly environment.

This is why it is essential that those who need to, take it slow in developing their psychic side. To do so quickly would be to introduce new stress into their already overburdened life. Their ability to cope depends upon shielding themselves from some psychic transmissions, particularly from their oversoul, which urges them to sustain themselves using much simpler means. They strive and move forward, and do not realize the alternatives that lay before them. Still, they could not fathom these spiritual truths at this time.

A part of them was introduced to the topic of manifestation, and they were fascinated. Yet, they also remained quiet and afraid. They decided that the whole topic was a sham, and definitely not for them. They turned away from the magical aspects of spirituality and concentrated upon the concreteness or orderly rules. In this respect, their own minds and lives were kept orderly and predictable.

In your zeal to share psychic gifts with one another, some of you will feel shame when you truly look at your lives with clear vision. It is easier to turn away and cloud your vision a little while longer than to be still and simply listen for guidance and direction. Be gracious when this occurs, and force not one person to look upon his or her holy self with judgmental eyes. Better to share your psychic gifts through prayerfulness than to push one person to look beyond the veil if they are not ready. For fear, which would startle them, is not appropriate in this dimension.

You who are blessed with eyes that are opened, gaze upon your hapless brothers and sisters with a loving outlook. See in them their truth, even if they cannot see this for themselves. Give them a push in the direction of Light, not by forcing their eyes to see, but by being a shining example of truth yourself. Admire everyone's beauty freely, and drink in the perfume of Spirit that is all around you. And use your psychic gifts to shower the world with Divine light.

You are given the ability to know many things that perhaps the average person cannot understand, or, more accurately, is unwilling to explore. Take your time to get to know your strengths, and do not seek to dazzle others with your abilities. Instead, use this gift as one more method of extending kindness and appreciation. Any tool that is used in this service is from the Light, indeed.

❧ Reincarnation ❧

Is there a process of rebirth where the child's soul has come from another part of the universe to be rejoined with certain factions whom he or she has known before? Why, certainly. This process need not surprise you, since you already marvel at the wondrous power of which God and humans are capable. Why should the soul be incapable of retreading itself through many lifetimes? The very nature of the universe has given humans power and dominion over their souls' destiny, including the ability to travel through time and space.

You see, reincarnation is but a small parcel of the entire project within the label of "human growth," as you call it. We merely term it "adventures of the soul," in which the human traits are attributed to the soul through a recycling of lifetimes. It marks time, offers excitement—as well as a good deal of experience that any soul may gain. It isn't "sinful," as some may fear. It is merely one more way to mark time, much as any decision is made during any given lifetime.

Each soul has experiences collected from this vast environment stored in their subconscious. Some are their own experiences; some are those gathered from others. In the subconscious, these experiences are all the same. They mark the forward movement of time, which is viewed as progress, and is pleasurable. Yet, the election to participate in the reincarnation process also has the flip-side effect of locking the soul into time, simply because the being is convinced that progression comes through marking time. This belief reinforces the attributes of time, and flattens their very abilities to escape it.

Some of you fear that a soul without a physical life is one without meaning or shape. Cast into a void, the nonphysical soul lives a gray and unaware existence, you fear. So you cling to your human shape, hoping that this will carve out some semblance of meaning and importance. You see yourselves as lacking, and you hope that through time, you will progress into one who lacks not. Yet, how could any creation of God want for anything? It is only a belief that the future will bring you goodness that entangles you into a mire of lack, a dependency on the "future," and a need for time measurement.

The escape from this trap is simple, yet you may feel confined by the reinforced measurement of time that you see mirrored around you. Rather than attempt to escape from time measurement, then, do train your mind to escape from self-judgments concerning lack. You do not lack anything, and you cannot afford to continue this self-judgment any longer! The human race must stop confusing material supply with human worthiness. You are worthy, and you *do* have everything.

If this confuses you (because your world seems to mirror otherwise), press forward still. Your Creator wills for you to have everything, now and for all of eternity. God sees that you have no needs and that you are supplied in every way. Yet, with your God-given power of creation, you can paint a picture of lack at your command. This gives you pleasure in some way, perhaps by allowing you to get along with your fellow humans, who seem so invested in this sense of lack—and the need for progress.

Your soul needs no progress, for it has never left God's side, and has never forgotten its holy self and wondrous gifts! By listening to your soul, you hear the echoes of this truth. You are supplied, you are home, and you are safe. Now.

‿ Romantic Love ‿

Although romantic love doesn't hold a candle to the brightness of the Divine flame of love, and doesn't come close to the comfort that is unparalleled from being cradled in God's Divine perfection, romantic love does pose a worthy substitute of sorts. First, it provides you with a sense of safety and protection. There are so many feelings of danger in this world, yes? So many times when a longing for safety and protection is satisfied only within your lover's arms.

Romantic love begins with a deluded sense of safety, which is then substituted for an additional sense of danger along the way. What we mean is this: You initially begin the course of your relationship with open-minded trust, and then you pick items from your discourse that remind you of danger. You analyze the details of your relationship, deciding upon this or that as indications that you are unsafe. You then embellish these feelings with unhappiness, feeling that, once again, all of your hopes are being dashed.

What you are really seeking within the context of a romantic love relationship is carelessness. A carefree attitude and spirit is the hope for all of God's creations. We do not mean that you would sidestep your responsibilities with carelessness—oh, no. We merely mean that you would cast your cares and worries to love, and trust in the power of the universe to carry you safely.

Your cares are wearisome, and they cause you great sorrow and heavy burdens. You seek a partnership where you can escape these encumbrances, if even momentarily. A respite from the constant turmoil and stress is essential to your soul's peace of mind. When a new relationship offers this escape, you, naturally, are blissful.

The balance in a romantic relationship is thus, then: to keep the relationship from adding to your burdens. So many partnerships explode and die when a perception occurs that this relationship is creating more feelings of danger than it is easing. For when additional stressors occur as a result of the relationship, the natural reaction is to seek shelter and safety. This is when most relationships get into trouble, for the partner seeks this shelter and safety outside of the relationship.

Only through casting your inevitable cares and worries to the true source of love, God, can a partnership remain on the highest plane possible. If the partners are willing to do this together, so much the better. Then, there is hope that romantic love will continue to be a shelter in the storm, instead of a mirage that cruelly offers sustenance that doesn't exist.

Romantic love is a frontage road, running parallel to the true path of God's Divine love. Romantic and Divine love can complement one another, as they are essentially from the same Source. Yet, when romantic love is sought as a replacement for Divine love, dissatisfaction always creeps in. Remember to bring a sense of the sacred into your romantic love relationship, and to seek for safety and shelter together in the only place that it can be found: in God within.

Self-Esteem

There is a part of your human consciousness that often criticizes you with harsh intent. It wounds your emotions and drags down the elevation with which you view yourself. When this happens, you neglect to notice your Godliness, and you may forget to see it within others. Grandiosity is also involved, as it elevates you to a place of "safety" where nothing concerns you and no one can harm you.

Elevations or disruptions in your Godly self-perception create crises within you, Beloved One. Forget not your Heavenly Creator, Who steadily resides within you now. There is no room for error on His part, and nothing that He created comes undone from its origin of perfection. This criticism that you suffer at your own hands is your own invention, designed to propel you from the heights of Heaven and cast you down into the bowels of self-suffering. And why would a Heavenly creation choose such a course as this? Experimentation is part of the design behind this decision. Creative suffering is a way for humans to extinguish their thirst to return home to Heaven. By placing yourself in a negative light, you effectively "forget" about your Heavenly home, and in that respect, you feel more settled in your Earthly home.

Yet, we are here to herald in a new and different way to extinguish your painful longings for home, Dearest Child of God! This pain, you can turn around, and use it to elevate yourself in consciousness to a new level of awareness of your truth. The "truth" that is within suffering is but a pinpoint upon a whole landscape of awareness that awaits you now. Learning through suffering is a slow and arduous task, while we stand idly by, ready to whisk you off to a conscious awareness of your inner truth.

You, who have such greatness in store for you, must not wait a moment more to grasp this option that is so readily available. Take it in hand, and cleave it tightly to your chest. For you are all-powerful, like your Creator, but in a different way. Your creations can be in the awakening to joy, when you choose to experience that joy for yourself. Your joy bubbles over, frothing outward, encouraging others much like a laugh catches on within a group. There is much opportunity for you now to promote this joy within and without, and you must forsake suffering and leave it behind.

Your "self-esteem" is simply an assessment of how you are spending this moment. It is similar to noting how you are spending your money, and whether you are respecting this valuable resource. As you suffer, you are disregarding the valuable opportunity of that moment, and negating choices of joy that are presently available. As you soar in laughter, you have respected your options and chosen wisely. This is true even when you are engaged in responsibilities that you would deem "serious." There is still room for laughter in your heart in each situation, no matter the context.

When you speak of high self-esteem, we know that you mean having great regard and respect for yourself. And we say that the route to this result is through regarding and respecting your resources of the moment *right now*. Fully squeeze the juice of joy from this moment, and you shall be gladdened that you made the decision that helps your inner self to rest peacefully.

You, who have the power of all of Heaven's spheres within your belly, have no need to ever disregard yourself. For, you are as holy as any of Heaven's creations. You are a shining example of God's handiwork, encapsulated in a being so lovely that all of Heaven breathes deeply at the sight of you. Do you not realize that we love you eternally, and that we work tirelessly to bring you through periods of restlessness, sorrow, and peril into the light of joy? Everything is built in your favor, Dear One, and we but await your decision to stand in the light of this joy.

~≈ Sexuality ≈~

Couplings are unions of the mind, body, and spirit, urged along by the desire for procreation and reunion with God. These intermingling desires are so strong that the urge for sex is among the most intense of all of the instincts. We shall look at the topic in this light.

Within all Earthly beings, there is an instinctual drive to procreate. That is so because the literal manufacture of additional beings depends upon such procreation tendencies. Without the urge, the various species would not bother to procreate, now, would they? The pleasure factor was necessary to build into this arena, again, to ensure the survival of the various species.

Outside of these basic instincts are those that are deeper still. Not better, just deeper. This drive is for reunion with the Godhead, which is the gathering of souls who are united as one with our Creator. You are presently a member of that Godhead, and you are at this moment joined with God and the Godhead. Yet, your ego has created a schism of awareness that blocks you from this realization.

The in-soul (the higher self), however, remembers this union, and seeks to return through the realization of oneness with God and the Godhead. The closest experiences upon the earth are found within meditation, prayer, and couplings. In coupling, there is a sense of closeness that verges on that of *joining* and *union*. The sexual organs are merged, and the heart-space is opened to one another. The physical space between the two hearts is close, which replicates a sense of oneness.

The bliss of this coupling pairs the physical intensity with a loss of time-awareness. When you lose track of time, your soul travels to a higher orbit where it can access glimpses of truth. Earthly laws no longer restrict the timeless soul, allowing you to literally glimpse the bliss of union—not only with your beloved, but also with the ultimate Beloved One, the Godhead.

Those moments when you feel the greatest urge to couple are when you are in the greatest need of reunion with God and the Godhead. Let it be known that you truly are at home with the Godhead at all times. Yet, when this truth is forgotten, coupling is an Earthly substitute that can bring your consciousness home.

～ Sleep ～

When you close your eyes and drift away, do you believe that your soul escapes the confines of Earthly life and momentarily wends its way Heavenward to replenish and remind? Yes, it is true, in case you wondered about this. Beloved One, these dreamtime travels are your solace and salvation in so many ways. They provide you with escape from harsh climates, a chance to examine them from afar, and a way to receive a fresh approach to life.

All we ask is that you trust that your travels are put together for prime reasons, and that no harm can come unto you. Your sleeptime is guaranteed to be infused with safety in all ways. What we mean is that no harm can come unto your body while we safeguard it during your passage-time. You vent during the escape, much like steam escaping and releasing pent-up pressure. Without this nightly escape, life could seem unbearable to you.

Often, you remember fragments of these soul escapes, and you wonder, *What do they mean?* Yet, although you cannot recall the particular details of the night's adventures, they serve their purpose well: First, they function as an escape valve, releasing built-up pressure within the system; second, these dreamtime sojourns provide you with conscious realization of your holy and Divine nature. These are opportunities for you to witness and experience your holy nature without prejudice or judgment on your part. You are beautifully open to us during these journeys, and it is only upon awakening that you may argue with your "logical mind" as to the reality of the experience. Yet, even with your logical mind's rejection, the experience is lodged within your subconscious, nonetheless. Your in-soul (higher self) is witness to Heaven's beauty each night, thereby refueling it for another Earthly day.

Sleep is refreshing due to these journeys, and you awaken feeling renewed because of this built-in pleasure. When you join us each dreamtime for a class or an assignment, we welcome you with open arms, and you melt into our embrace. It is as if you are starving for affection most times that we connect in this way. And perhaps that is the greatest value of the sleeptime of all: a chance for you to witness life's most amazing miracle: love—feeling it, drinking it in, replenishing yourself, and reminding you of your holy origin. Sleep well, Beloved One. We'll see you in your dreams!

⊰ Soulmate ⊱

There is more truth to the term *soulmate* than some would realize. For a soulmate is literally a mate from your soul-group, a being who has been furnished to you as an Earthly guide, even as you are furnished to him or her. You must recall, at the deepest level, that your origin is not of the earth. It is of that stratosphere that you term as "Heaven," in which souls reside. Some of these souls create close-knit bonds, forming companionships, clusters, and groups in some instances. These assemblies vary in size and dimension, depending upon the common interests of the beings concerned.

These beings become "mates," in the sense of companions and comrades. They depend upon each other for guidance and advice. When a mate branches off and opts for a lifetime upon a planet, it is common for another mate to volunteer to accompany him or her along the way. A recognition of a soulmate when you are upon Earth is an exciting moment. There is a degree of familiarity with such a person that is unearthly.

Yet, this is not to be confused with a desire for a close-knit love bond with a romantic partner who will be your perfect mate. The fact that your soulmate is bonded to you is undeniable. Yet, it does not automatically follow that this soulmate will be bound to you for a lifetime. This person comes to you to comfort you, and to bring you solace from home. He or she comes to watch over you, to remind you of your Earthly lessons, and to bring you Earthly gifts. Yet, it would be a logical fallacy to believe that this could be "the one" for which you seek in your romantic fantasies.

"The One," in the sense of the world's meaning, is quite illusory. It is a romantic notion, to be sure, and one that many do find, and even more chase after. Yet, "the One" does not equate to a soulmate, necessarily. For a soulmate is what you might instead term a "helpmate"— that is, one who helps you to accomplish the mission that you elected to attain in this lifetime. Your soulmate is literally a friend from home, sent to give you recognition of the One who is your Source and your Creator. Your soulmate helps you to recall the One's light and everlasting love.

When you are attracted to a soulmate, you are attracted to God's qualities that you see within that being. When you love a soulmate, you are literally loving God.

Each partnership comes to you for a specific reason and purpose, and you will feel a tugging at your heart toward your Beloved. This tugging is the very pull of the purpose behind the partnership. The goal of the partnership may be fulfilled within minutes or within decades. But one thing is certain: When the purpose has been served, the pull of the relationship will subside. The partners may say that they are "turned off," yet the truth is that they are now off to serve another purpose and will likely be united with new partners. Their love will never dissolve, and gratitude is owed to one another for the important part in which they each participated. Then, it is time to stop looking back, and to be committed to serving the purpose in the current moment.

You may meet and love many soulmates, Dear One, depending upon your soul-group's size and dimensions. Some of your soulmates are yet in spirit, awaiting an Earthly birth. You will teach many of them during your Earthly time, and you will also learn from them as well. And ultimately, your return to your soul-group is marked with happiness and joy. Why not enjoy that happiness and joy now, while you are with these great beings sent to you from Home?

When you meet a soulmate, do not seek to capture this person, but enjoy and delight in their Heavenly gifts. Drink them in to fuel yourself for your Earthly mission. Whether or not this partnership culminates in union is not what matters. It is the process of seeing Heaven reflected in their holy eyes and having this vision mirrored back to you of your own Divine self that truly is important. Soulmates, you are blessed indeed. We angels kiss you with gratitude, as you shine upon one another His holy and Divine grace and love.

❧ Stress ❧

Wherever you find stress, you will also find feelings of victimhood. Anger at being forced beyond one's willingness is the essence of stress. The tension is spurred by underlying resentment toward misperceived authorities—misperceived because no one has authority over you. No one can force you—no one but your own powerful self. All stress is self-imposed, since all stress-inducing situations are elected by your own free will. There are no exceptions, because in all doings, you have the choice to remove yourself from the stressful situation. While it is true that certain consequences would follow, it still holds true that your options are always freely available to you.

Dear Ones, the truth concerning stress is that you choose pain when you are afraid of delving into your holy life purpose. Pain is a time deceiver, covering the holes in your schedule that ache to be devoted toward your life's purpose. When you are unsure of yourself, your abilities, your strengths, and your very gifts, you divert yourself with pain. Stress is perhaps the most common that we see among you, for this pain is elective, acceptable, and socially reinforced.

Have no shame, though, as shame is among the most painful of the stressors that you carry. It is wounding and prohibitive, preventing you from experiencing your Divine power. Shame-stress cloaks your light, blinding you to your God-self. And thus, you feel incapable of contributing to the world.

When you feel stress, call upon us angels, and allow us to open the doors of the self-made prisons that you have barred yourself behind. Allow us to drop your defenses, your sense of unworthiness. Allow us to fan the flames of your Divine light so that you can step up to your life's purpose without hesitation, without delay, and without compromise.

Stress is not your prisoner. You are. Imprison yourself no longer, for you are a Holy Child of the Power. You are born to take this power out into the world and experience it as the life-changing force that brings great joy to many. You are meant to move forward in large, sweeping motions; and subtle, soft breaths. You cannot stop the movement of God's child with the illusion of imprisonment, no more than you can contain the sparks of the sun. As you catapult outwardly, release any fears or doubts to us angels. In that way, you will not need the shield of stress to "protect" you from any harm that may be involved in fulfilling your life's purpose. Only the ego fears that your purpose will harm you, and it offers to shield you from this "harm" with diversions.

No matter that you are unsure of the direction or outcome that this mission calls you toward. No matter that you have no explicit guarantee of success except your soul's ceaseless beckoning. Your soul knows that uncovering its natural happiness lies in extending its happiness outwardly, like a spring bubbling forth with its precious gift of water. As you flow forward, you naturally avoid situations that would deter or delay you. You have that choice, and you have the ability to choose now.

We seek to remind you that you have always been able to cope with each situation that has presented itself to you. This is as true of your future as it is of your past. There is no danger lurking in a corner, ready to pounce upon you. Yet, this fear of controlling your future is a large contributor to your stress, is it not? You must trust that you will be ready each moment for whatever comes along. You will not perish, be abandoned, or starve in any way. All will be provided for you on your path. Oh, yes, you will have your role in the responsibility for this alignment, to be sure.

But allow us to reassure you once again that there is nothing coming your way that you won't be able to withstand. Always, we will hold your hand steadily and guide you. How could we not help you to traverse your many passages? We are your angels, and we love you so.

Many will suffer along the way, and you will witness their pain and implore us, "Why must this be?" And we say to you that you are sent to them to witness their suffering and to alleviate their pain. You are not to absorb their suffering, no—but to shelter them from additional storms by offering them the only solace that we have available: love.

Whenever you extend pity, you reinforce the suffering. But whenever you extend compassion and love, you end the suffering. Pity sees the suffering as a mirror of victimhood. And if you see people as victims, how are they to escape without valiant efforts from a supernatural force? You thus reinforce their sense of powerlessness, which crushes the very knowledge that will help them escape. With powerlessness, they must reach for help with every trial that they manifest. They become weak, dependent, and fearful.

So much better to reinforce their inner power than their sense of powerlessness! Take them by the hand and lead them home by showing them the strength within. Reveal it to them by recounting examples of their courage, their temperance, their wisdom, and their kindness. Remind them of their own fortitude, and help them to feel their own power grow.

In this way, they can feel strong and interdependent once again. They see the power within their own grace, and this self-perception is reflected in the power within the angels around them. They represent a powerful center amidst a powerful and benevolent universe. This knowledge helps them so that they can help others. So, you see that you do the world so much good when you lift someone's spirit through this process of empowerment, and yet you continue to query: "Why? Why is there suffering when God is all-loving and powerful?" And we say that this is among the mysteries of the universe that is little understood. And still we try to explain gently that, yes, our Creator is a mighty and powerful essence of the all-encompassing Love. This love is so bright that it deflects all darkness. It doesn't fight the darkness. Nor does the light fight the dark. Darkness simply is unable to penetrate the intensely bright glare of the One. It is literally cast away by the beaming brightness.

Since no darkness can permeate the bright, the One does not experience darkness in any form. The One only knows light, and all of its forms: joy, peace, happiness, and unity. The One does not experience any form of darkness, including suffering. This does not mean that God ignores suffering or shows favoritism. It simply means that the One deputizes you to bring light to all situations of darkness. Be as the Creator, and shine light upon any situation that is not built upon a foundation of joy. In this way, you act as the Earthly angel who forms a bridge of light, allowing others to come home.

≈ Twin Flame ≈

With the increasing focus upon love in your world, it is no wonder that there is also a corresponding curiosity abut the forms that love can take within human relationships. Chief within the "prizes" of love that you seek is the holy grail of soulmate loves: what you term your "twin flame."

The quest for a twin is an ancient one. It is a desire for validation that who you are is lovable. If you were to find one who mirrored yourself completely, and you loved one another, this would satiate your fears of ego origin. Your ego haunts you with questions as to your self-worth, and the idea of a twin flame provides you with hope that you are wholly lovable.

First, let us assure you that—with or without a soulmate, or with or without a twin flame in your vicinity—you *are* wholly lovable! You, who are the grandest example of love in the universe, are built upon the wings of love. You are appreciated and desired by all that is holy, and it is your holy brethren who speak, in a voice barely distinguishable from the wind, of your mirrored existence. For you see that all beings, as such, are your twins, your brothers, your sisters, your flames.

It is a special flame that you seek, to be sure, and we do not seek to mock or overstate this principle. We are here to encourage love, not to dissuade you. You are here, to begin with, to experience love in all its grandest forms. And love's sweet kiss swells your heart like no other. We are your admirers, and we can bring you to the partnership you deeply desire.

The concept of a twin flame was engendered long ago. The pod from which your soul imparted itself before traversing to Earth has many components. They are your family of origin of sorts, although the truth is that *all* who exist are part of you. There were close bonds forged within your soul pod in Heaven, nonetheless. And just as experiences shape your personality and destiny while you are here, so too do shared experiences create similarities in outlooks within groups in general. A basic example are two children who share a household and have life experiences together, which cause them to share certain opinions.

In the soul pod within Heaven's sphere, the same principle applies. A twin flame is akin to a best friend upon Earth, and is one who so closely resembles you in thought and deed that you fall in love with your "self" through his or her eyes. This is a being who has shared rich experiences with you—some in this lifetime, some in your past. At times, you may have looked over one another as a "spirit guide." These relationships steered you both in similar directions through your shared experiences in Heaven and upon Earth. That is why it is not uncommon for twin flames, upon rejoining one another in adulthood, to have remarkably similar histories to one another.

Will you meet your twin flame in this lifetime, you ask? Your question stems from your true underlying desire to feel wholly loved. And we remind you once again to begin your quest with a full cup, and not one that hungers for love. A desperate fear accompanies one who feels empty, and such fear is not a quotient for attracting the love that you seek. Prayer, meditation, yogic stretching, communion with like-minded souls, quiet reposes in nature . . . all are means to the end which you seek: a fulfillment of love.

Once your desire for this love is quenched in the proper manner, through the inpouring of realizing God's enormous love that is within you now, you shall find the reflections of this love in your Earthly experiences. You shall have love in such great quantities that it is as if Heaven has poured giant buckets of love from a ceaseless well! Friends will smile and laugh with you, and you shall not feel lonely or unloved again.

You *do have* great love within you at this very moment. Realizing this treasure trove quenches you so completely that your light beams across and upward through the cosmos. Miracles rush toward those who love so completely, and if you accept love through a human relationship, it shall be yours indeed.

Yoga

We have already talked with you about the importance of breath, exercise, and meditation, and we do not mean to nag you about this subject. That is why yoga is presented to you as a route to establish all of these conditions within a short timespan. When you engage in the practice of yoga, the rejuvenation establishes within you a great surge of energy. Establishing your yogic practices within a specific schedule makes the habit become second nature, which we highly recommend. We do urge you to consider some form of yoga practice, however that may come. For some, it will be on a casual basis, while others will consider it to be a necessary part of their lifeblood.

Yogic practices were introduced long ago, and are only recently awakening in your lands. The practice now comes to you with an accumulation of prayers behind it—a force so great that by immersing yourself in its radiance, great transformation can take place. Those who originally practiced yoga sent prayers forward in time, asking that all who forever afterward conducted yoga, would receive those prayers. When you engage in the practice of yoga, you are immersed in the river flow of those ancient prayers.

You who are intimidated by the extent of your flexibility, hear our call: The yogic practice is a silent path that enriches you from within. Use it as a measure to center yourself peacefully, and not as a route to establish your "inferiority" or "superiority" to another.

Lest you think that we chastise you on this count, please know that we oversee the yogic practice as a sacred art, and not a measurement of competition. You are perfectly aligned in all ways now, and the natural extension is to bathe your awareness with the flood of breath that comes as you stretch and bend.

Delay not your yogic practice a moment longer, Dearest One, for we see countless benefits upon you from this act. We will bring to you situations and teachers who can anchor your yogic practice and instill into you this new and lasting habit of deep and cleansing breath, mixed with periodic stretching.

Within each moment of stillness, there lies a hearty action awaiting your connection. Through stillness, you cease to flood your mind with information that competes for your awareness. Through this stillness, you hear our words carried upon the silence of your breath. Be glad, then, that this extension of Heaven's love comes to you through daily yogic postures. You, who are scheduled so tightly that you cannot bear to add to your load of duties, this is a call to greater awareness through instilling a yogic practice. It is a miraculous example of receiving more through giving, in that the greater your devotion to your yogic practice, the more you do receive.

Think us not callous or uncaring when referring to your time schedule, Dear One. We merely tap you on the shoulder quite gently with our words, urging you tenderly toward that which you already know to be true, for at all moments, your free will shines like a beacon on the horizon. We do not seek to, nor can we, bend that light to suit any will but your own, which is truly one part of God's will. For you will find your own way unto your retreat in stillness, and we offer you our words as a gift to you now. We do see your outcome with each choice that you make, and we seek only to encourage you whenever possible to make the choice for happiness in all ways.

PART II

Messages from
the Archangels

A Message from
Archangel Michael

Q: Archangel Michael, what would you like to say to us?

A: Sit quietly, breathe deeply, and open your crown chakra so that I may have a vessel in which to pour my information and deep love and respect for you. So often you run away from meeting me face-to-face for fear of what I might say. Fear not, because I come in the name of the Host of all planets and beyond! I am in charge of the "light brigade," and the situation upon Earth needs us all at this very moment. During times of great strife and peril, whom do you suppose it is who holds the structure together like glue? It is our shared light, which permeates even situations of grave danger. There is truly nothing to fear, as you have the miraculous ability to ride upon this plane of light and escape danger of any form.

So sit back and quietly reach an awareness of this great light that is within and around you right now. Meditate upon the intention of knowing this light. It has power greater than any forces humankind has ever created. It is the secret of the universe, the cause and the power of great resolve. This light, Dear and Beloved One, is a mighty and invincible force that can never be eradicated or taken away. It is limitless, and reaches from where you are right now to the far reaches of the universe. It is timeless, and in the blink of an eye, it can cover an entire planet.

Keep implanting this light wherever your human eye gazes upon sorrow. Show your vigilance for peace by showering the earth with your Divine and holy light. Make no mistake about it: You are among the foot soldiers of Divine Truth and awareness, and you truly make a difference when you cast your eye on this hidden ability of healing power. Bring forth miracles, Beloved One, by shooting light from your heart, your mind, and your head, showering and blanketing all the many dimensions with this gift of light.

Like a healing salve shall it soothe and heal away all ill will. The light can be a variety of colors, as you choose and are guided. For instance, pouring pale blue light on an angry situation will extinguish the flames of rage, like water drenching smoldering flames. Dark blue light calms nerves and elevates the consciousness. You will witness dark blue light creating sleepy, philosophical discussions. There are so many other colors, and you shall want to experiment with each and note the effects thereof. Pink light, as you may imagine, engenders friendship and romantic love, and generally brings people closer together in fondness. Yellow light stimulates a working environment and helps those who are easily distracted to remain more focused upon their higher self's messages and guidance. As I say, go forth and experiment with these shining lights that can never backfire or be mistaken. Or, if there is a need for multidimensional healing, simply use white light, as it does contain all of the colors, especially my beloved purple, which is at the highest elevation of the spectrum. Purple light always helps people to shine at their highest state so that they unfold their inner wisdom in all ways. It stimulates the senses and adrenals, and creates a take-charge energy in which these high senses are used meaningfully.

So, do you see why I say that I am the leader of the "light brigade"? You, who are among countless members of this inner society, have much work to do. First, you need to awaken your sleeping brothers and sisters by shining your light at all times that you can remember to do so. Their inner light, like your own not too long ago, is sleeping—much like their consciousness. Feeling the sting of an illusion of trapped victimhood, they spin their wheels without going forward. Oh, how they need your shining love at this very moment to escape the trenches in which they lay! Help them to reach their highest state, Dear One, by being a shining example of a life lived in truth.

I need you to be vigilant for peace in all ways, and to stand for peacefulness in all of your doings. Within your own family system, settle for nothing less than a lively form of peacefulness within yourself. What this means is a quiet excitement, and nothing like the common definition of peacefulness that is more akin to "apathy." Peace is stimulating and quite exciting when truly experienced and understood. It means that you feel the faith that all matters are absolutely taken care of by the Divine Creator. Peacefulness means having the courage to always love, without fear of repercussion. It means taking charge of your day's events, in a way that leads you across the threshold of your passions. So, if your interests lead you to a library, a phone call, a "chance" meeting, or a walk, you will trust this leadership ability of your holy self and will.

I come to you often in your dreamtime travels, and I often lead you to see the assignments that you have asked for and have agreed to take on. That is why you so often have the feeling that you label "déjà vu," as you have had previews of your most pressing and vital operations before they occur. When you have these feelings of prior experiences, like recalling a dream through some daytime memory trigger, allow yourself to float timelessly, and connect with me even briefly. I will send you a signal that it is I who am with you, either through a flashing light that you shall see, or a palpable sensation that I am standing near you. You may experience this sensation as a type of wrapping around your head, or as a pressure upon your shoulders.

Either way, be not alarmed, for it is our preagreed signal that allows you to ferret out the importance of the situation. It is an opportunity for you to shed fear and to plant joy. Be assured that you are immensely qualified for this operation of peace, and that I stand beside you always, eternally, showering you with immense quantities of love and devotion. For I am Michael, direct from God, sent to show you your light in all ways.

A Message from
～ Archangel Raphael ～

Q: Archangel Raphael, what would you like to say to us?

A: So often you call upon me for physical healings, and rightly so, for I am destined to perform this function in the physical universe. And yet, I am equipped to do so much more, and it is this that I would like to share with you today. Disorder in the universe is impossible, but a perception of disorder is very commonplace.

When you perceive chaos in any form, be it a mess in your home or financial disarray, you are confounding the principle of order by which the universe operates. You see, so much of this principle requires your cooperation in order for you to enjoy its sustenance power. You cannot create chaos, but you can engender chaotic effects by judging a situation as being out of control. Your judgment sweeps you into disarray, thus rendering you outside the normal laws of order and control. Once outside of these laws, you perceive additional chaos, which lends itself to your despair, or what you call "stress." This is the root of all illness, Brothers and Sisters. This is the root of all suffering and pain.

Nothing can be disordered in this universe, but you can think it so. And your tremendous power of thought can render your life as disordered simply because that is your wish. How can you undo God's law of complete order, you may ask? And the answer is quite simple: You cannot. However, you can render the law useless simply because your perceptions are beyond it. You see chaos, and thus experience it as "stress." Where there is Divine order, you see something else. Where there is perfect peace, you see disruption. Where there is health, you see sickness. And thus, you will see a different universe from the one your Maker created for you. And what you see, truly *is* what you get.

No matter that your misperception is but illusion. In your world, you think it is quite real indeed. And so you call upon me and my brethren angels to take care of matters, which is something we are quite willing and accustomed to doing. Can you see, though, that this is the long road to complete wellness? With just an inkling of perception toward Divine order, chaos can no longer reign.

When you gaze upon disorder, then, call upon us angels to ascribe to you a different consciousness—one of perfect peace. We will assist you, if you will allow us to, in resigning to a different view of your world. You will see the perfect plan behind everything, even the seeming chaos. You will see the mathematical precision with which everything is orchestrated—the balance, the timing, the everything.

And thus will you see great beauty, within and without. You will marvel at the splendor that is before you eternally—not just now, but always. Your breath will draw deeply in awe, and you shall be gladdened that it is so.

The route to perfect health, then, begins with a single breath. It happens at the most unlikely time, when you are saddened over some misperceived event. That is the moment to take inventory of your perceptions! Say to yourself over and over, "This *cannot* be so!" Deny the fact of chaos's existence, and claim the truth of God's abiding plan of love. Know that disarray cannot enter God's universe, and your perception of disarray shall be erased to the degree that you allow it. A complete and utter healing will be revealed with this change of attitude. You might call healing, then, an "attitude adjustment," if I may be so bold.

Think not that I disrespect the human condition of sadness, nor that I am callous about human suffering. Quite the opposite, Dearest Ones! I am heralding in a new age of perception, one in which dimness gives way to the brightest sunlight imaginable, where grief and sadness are healed the instant that recognition of God's holy plan is enacted, where broken bones are mended in the instant of this recognition, and where lives that have been disordered are put back into place where they belong: on God's beautiful mantel along with all of His treasures of creation. It is pristinely perfect in all ways—that is His doing—and you no longer stand outside of this beauty with your holy perception intact once again.

You are already healed, and I am here as a guardian angel so that your perceptions remain in this healed position. When you step outside of the knowledge of your holiness, ask me to help you step back inside, like a Heavenly dance instructor. The movement is simple; it is your willingness to change your perception that often is difficult for you to conjure. You do have many miraculous abilities, which are only limited by your own forgetfulness. Let this be the time and the place of your increased willingness to allow miracles to be conveyed through your perception of light and order, seeing these things upon all that you gaze.

A Message from
~ Archangel Uriel ~

Q: Archangel Uriel, I feel as if I don't know you as well as the other angels. Your personality doesn't seem as distinct. What would you like to tell us about yourself and your role, and what messages do you have for us?

A: I am glad that you invited me to join you in the writing of this book, Doreen, for I have long been hovering over many of your projects, and although I may seem elusive and difficult to pinpoint, my presence has always been with you. I beam light into many situations where you perceive difficulty, helping you to untangle them in the same way that your hair-conditioning cream helps to untangle your hair. I respectfully stay out of the realm of speaking to you directly in most instances, preferring instead to stay behind the scenes, where I can offer the most help during times of difficulty.

My love for you is constantly outpouring from my heart to yours (and I mean this for every human who could possibly hear these words as well). I am kept so busy, constantly pouring love on situations, in the manner of a fireman in a searing forest fire who is busily extinguishing the bitterly raging blaze. I extinguish pain in situations where despair seems to reign so that you can see and think clearly in order to escape the situation. I bring new light into your consciousness so that hope may return to your heart. In many ways, I help you to access the creative solutions that the Divine mind constantly offers you, but which you cannot receive without a clear mind.

I am the window washer of your outlook, then. I simply remove the clouds so that you may see life through a new lens. Many times you have referred to me as the "psychologist angel," and that is mostly correct. I do have the ability to create a change of heart and engender forgiveness—even in the most unlikely situations where hate or rage are smoldering beyond all comprehension. I cool the flames of hatred and bring one back to the awareness of their own Divine love. And yet, it is limiting to think of me only as the Archangel of Forgiveness, when there is so much more that I can do to help humanity and beyond.

For one thing, I am among the newer of the archangels upon the human scene. The other archangels, many of whom you have already met (and some of whom are on their way to meet you in your conscious awareness), have, as you call it, more "distinctive" personality traits that make them instantly recognizable. Michael, with his unerring sword, is a powerful contender for your consciousness. Who could ignore his booming voice and commanding spirit? Raphael, with his eternal sweetness and eager helpfulness, is akin to a best friend whom you would always want by your side. And Gabriel is the ever-present helper to those with brilliant and creative minds, channeling this creativity into helpfulness upon the earth. And who am I, in this scope of archangeldom? I am the one who is willing to help from afar, the one who "fuels" each situation of healing with my willingness to pour large streams of light into your mind and onto the situation.

This light is the very lifeblood of healing, since it opens your mind and heart to see the situation from a new perspective. The infusion of my floodlight helps you to step back and think again. It assists you in preparing your heart for forgiveness, even as your head screams for revenge. It skips over the attack reflex and cushions you from automatic reflexes of revenge. In this way, you don't soften in a way that you might deem being a "fool." You soften in a way that gives you new resolve, insight, and strength.

Think of me, then, as you would a wise uncle who offers a new perspective in troubling situations. I bring to you eons of wisdom, garnered from the very tapestry of life itself. And yet, my greatest bequeathment comes in the form of the greatest of riches: my urn of light, which I pour gladly upon your holy head whenever it is bowed in sorrow. My urn is eternally filled with a renewal of light, and I have endless time with which to spend with you.

And not only is this light a healing catalyst, but it is also filled with the properties of our endless conversations, which occur at such a high frequency that your consciousness is often unaware. These are the times I enjoy the most: the high-level frequencies that are our "chats," our "get-togethers," and that often occur within your meditations, your dreams, and times of your open expansiveness. The profundities that we share during these unseen conversations are most enjoyable to me, and my heart leaps with joy as I witness you penciling down these thoughts, capturing their wisdom for your own enjoyment and prosperity.

Seek me out often, for I am working overtime on your behalf. Think not that I shall tire of your companionship, for my duty is to you. I relish our time spent together in conversation, and I am equally at ease during those times of your unawareness of my mission. I am the Light, as are you, and together, our pooling of light brings much joy to the entire universe.

A Message from
～ Archangel Gabriel ～

Q: Archangel Gabriel, what message would you like to share with us?

A: You know that I am the angel who engenders communication of the deepest variety. My overriding function is to enable you to speak truthfully, while feeling at peace with the process. I see many of you expanding the scope of your horizon, wherein you are now more aware of Spirit. You are assimilating these changes rapidly, and I am heralding you for your courage!

Much of my work involves shepherding you along, wherein I coax you to be free of lies, deceit, and half-truths—first, toward yourself. You cower in fear and loneliness, unwilling to seek freedom and peace through speaking your truth. That is where I come into play. I am your powerful ally in your attempts to speak up for yourself. But I must remind you once again that first you speak up *to* yourself, and then you speak up *for* yourself.

Truth-telling must begin within your own being, where you allow yourself a period of chaos and confusion while you sort through the many types of confusion that inevitably follow a close inventory of your life's picture. So often you wait for some far-off future day to carefully inspect your life, worried that such an inventory will cause you to toss overboard everything that you deeply value. You will not be so careless,

Holy One, but you will become confused by various and conflicting desires. There is no way out of this condition, but through truth-telling, and I will repeat myself: *first, truth-telling to yourself.*

When you take a clear-eyed and honest inventory of your present-day situation, you are imbued with the power to address all concerns. But when you remain bleary-eyed with procrastination, your own self takes a back seat and suffers the wounds of self-abuse. You do not deserve secondary treatment of any form! Raise your standards considerably this day, and fear not that conditions will become so chaotic that you are overwhelmed with grief.

Truth-telling to yourself does not equate to having to throw everything that matters overboard. Oh, no! It is a process that equalizes the imbalances that have thrown you off-center. You have stuffed many secrets into your closets, unwilling to expose them to your own self. What do you suppose this secret-keeping does to you? Think of how secrets adversely affect any relationship, and you shall know the answer. Whenever we create barriers within our sphere of awareness, saying, "No, I shalt not look there!" we compartmentalize ourselves. We become split in our awareness and divided in our loyalties. Union with your own self requires rejoining those split awarenesses, and although this may sound lofty and complicated, it is simple still. I am here as your guide, leading you through the traverses of self-awareness.

You fear looking within because you harbor fears of what you may find there. You fear finding darkness, you fear making changes based upon your inventory, and you fear self-loathing due to what you may find. All of these fears cause you to run and hide from your very own self. You, who are forever linked with your Holy Self, though, cannot truly hide. You know that there is a part of your self that is very holy. You also know that there is a part of your self that is capable of dark and dastardly schemes. This schism causes you to avoid looking inward, cloaking you instead with busyness and endless tasks that keep you enshrouded in a choked schedule.

I will lead you past the darkness, and show you to the light that dwelleth within you, Holy Angel! I will hold you with loving firmness so that you shall not be afraid when you gaze upon your Holy Self. I will take you to heights that you can only imagine, if you will but trust me for a while. The truth shall cast away all of your fears, as I gently guide you to look inwardly with loving honesty.

This merely means assembling a list of that which no longer honors you in your life. This list may include characteristics that you would like to shed; or it may include persons, places, or conditions that no longer serve your sacred mission. It may mean moves, changes, and new plans. Do not let this frighten you, Holy One! I will lead you along the way. Together, we are gathering the light of happiness into a fresh spring bouquet that we will share with the world.

In your world, you discuss "eliminating clutter," and this is rightly so. The energy clings to the old, sticking you to the past like glue. And similarly, you must be willing to eliminate the clutter from your very essence, trusting that new light will be shed on each area that you are willing to heal. For healing does not mean "discard." You need not throw away your relationships—just your relationship patterns! You need not toss out your home or material possessions—just the way in which they crowd you as if *they* owned you! Your reorganization is a call to greater freedom, through your willingness to speak your truth about those areas in which you feel crowded or controlled.

When you speak up to yourself, first in consciousness, and then in total awareness, the next steps easily follow. The difficult part is past, and new doors then open. As you strengthen yourself with this refreshing wave of self-honesty, your integrity permeates every aspect of your life. You shine more brightly in all of your partnerships, and others see your love beaming from your eyes. This is the love that comes from proper self-care, Holy One, and that is borne by your having the courage to face yourself and your life and say, "What is the truth here?"

PART III

A Message from
the Nature Angels

◦❧ The Nature Angels Speak ❧◦

You often refer to us as the fairies, devas, and elementals, but these are not our labels; they are yours. And while it is true that there are distinctions between us, there are fewer differences than there are similarities. The largest quantifying factor is that we all share this same Earthly dimension, and we must seek cooperative ways of maintaining the planet in more harmonious ways. Perhaps you may not realize what an earth-shattering problem many of your large corporations have created with their industrial waste and fumes. They have denied their involvement in this pollution, but we are witnesses to their devious ways. And while we do not seek to have this be a tome that preaches disillusionment or finger-pointing, we do require your involvement in ridding Earth of her harrowing pain.

First, there is the obvious Earthly pollution that comes from runoffs that are pointed toward our oceans, rivers, and streams. Being educated about these problems, and then having the courage to stand up and be vocal in transmuting them into more ecologically sound systems, is vital to our survival! Do not discount yourself, thinking, *Who am I? I am just one small person,* when you have so much good that you could do by visiting a single city council meeting! All of Earth is counting upon your voice—being heard through a face-to-face meeting or a written letter!

The knowledge is already in place as to a more ecological means to establish your systems. We gave this knowledge to your sensitive scientists long ago, yet they are hesitant to be vocal in the face of big business who insists that these systems will not work. Their true motivation, as you may guess, is profitability at the expense of pollution. They are not "evil" or "bad" in the traditional sense; they have just mastered the art of rationalization to the "nth" degree. They truly believe that the runoff and pollution that they engender will be fixed at a later time, and that it will then be somebody else's problem. They are squashed with financial responsibilities that cause them to seek more of the bottom line rather than do that which is right by the environment. Believe us, these corporate officers are painfully aware of what they do. We remind them nightly, while they sleep. That is why so many of them medicate themselves beyond comprehension—to stop the intruding voice of environmental reason from encroaching upon their slumber.

And yet, we mustn't seek to fuel the situation with our anger. For the second form of pollution largely fueled by large corporations comes from the cold atmosphere that repels even their key employees. All of the dissatisfaction that comes from someone dreading a job at a corporation, whether it be a "head honcho" or an "underling," is poisonous fuel that is poured daily into the earth's atmosphere, and which chokes her very being with its heavy gravity. You, who care deeply for planet Earth and her survival, can do much for the situation simply through monitoring your thoughts and purging them of dissatisfaction. We aren't suggesting that you bury your head in the sand and ignore your sadness or anger—no, not at all! We simply urge you to channel these feelings in a way that no longer harms the environment. For, the second biggest source of pollution comes from the minds of those who are dissatisfied. Nothing is dirtier, from our perspective, than the soot of a mind that is resentful! The filth permeates your Earth plane, from the oxygen level right down to the earth plates.

On the other hand, though, gratitude is akin to the most awesome of sunsets and sunrises. It is a dew-dropped flower, a kitten's meow, and all things that you consider most beautiful upon planet Earth.

We are here in stewardship of this great planet, and we have much to be grateful for. So, with a heart filled with love and resourcefulness, let us approach the situation with a calm, cool vision. Let us make our voices heard above the din of corporate greed. Let us take personalized steps toward cooling the rage upon the planet. Each of our own contributions counts enormously in the march toward a cleaner Earth!

As you gaze upon nature, or better yet, as you walk among us in the trees, plants, and flowers, ask us for daily assignments if you will. We will guide you successfully to tasks that take on the utmost importance in our environmental cause. We will open doors for you, and cause others to take note of your activities. Worry not about the attention this will bring you, for we will stand steadfastly by your side. We are magicians by nature, and we will teach our secrets to you gladly.

We have the greatest respect for humans such as yourself who use their Godly power in such noble ways. Fear not that others will misunderstand you. As we have said, we will be there, orchestrating much of the event! Trust us to handle the behind-the-scenes activities so that others will heed your word and deed. Your power will shine for others to see, and they will take note and emulate your take-charge stance. Thus, you will inspire others to be leaders of the environment, and you shall be glad for your contribution, which is of such great importance at this time.

Always stay in contact with nature, Lovely One, and wander not too far away from plants, birds, and trees, for your cities that are devoid of nature are in peril, as they offer us no place to live. When buildings and roads devour nature, that is a place that is dead, indeed. Be not surprised, then, if the deadness decays and falls. Even the city parks are oversprayed with insecticides, rendering them deadened wilderness! Seek out only places where nature truly sprawls in uncontrolled ways, for there you shall find plenty of us friends. We, like all ecosystems, are the glue that holds environments together. When we are ousted through overbuilding and pesticides, you shall see an imbalance in the community.

So, keep nature close by, even with potted plants and shrubs that you allow to grow wild. Visit us often, and speak to us like close friends and neighbors. As you communicate with us, through your mind or even aloud, you can feel our reply in your belly and hear it in your mind. We speak loudly to you, and you mustn't discount our urgent messages for fear that we are mistaken in choosing you. We *need* you! You are the one whom other humans will listen to, and by working as a team, we can bring this chapter of humanity to a close and never deal with pollution again.

PART IV

The Angels
Answer Your Questions

❧ Questions and Answers ❧

Q: So many times I can feel the presence of my angels, and I know that they're trying to tell me something, but I can't tell what the message is. How can I better hear my angels?

A: Trusting in your heart is a challenge that puzzles you at times. You hesitate to believe the heartstrings that tug at you to change your life and to improve your outlook. You hesitate because you doubt your own power and view yourself with a lens of littleness. You, who are the most powerful being in the universe, have diminished your own strength through this shortsightedness.

When you refuse to believe in your God-given gifts, how can we angels penetrate the barrier that this necessarily throws up? We permeate your thoughts with loving kindness, yet we cannot thrust our goodwill upon you.

Beloved One, you sometimes doubt whether a good life is part of your picture. Yet, why would one of God's beloved children deserve otherwise? For a sense of deservingness is at issue here. Do not doubt for an instant your power to evoke a great turnabout in your life by elevating your sense of self.

We do not bring this up to dissuade you from humbleness or

humility, for we speak not about grandiosity. The sense of separation that makes you doubt your own will being joined with His is a variety of grandiosity. You elevate yourself above or below God's creation by viewing yourself as apart from your glorious brothers or sisters. Do you truly believe that God would create you different from their making?

If you see a gift within one of your spiritual siblings, then it must be necessarily true that you have that gift available to you as well. Be grateful for those who have opened the door before you, for they have shown you new possibilities. You can endure goodness in your life by understanding that your life is not of your own making. You were created, and God did so for good reason. The expansion of His kingdom comes through your radiating presence, your light shining its beams outwardly in greater circles of manifestation.

As you accept your Godliness, you will naturally then accept our presence as your angels. We orbit you much like you see the stars in the sky hovering nearby planets. It is at that time, Beloved One, that your heart will open like a large expanse of light and allow us in. That is when you will allow yourself to clearly hear our singing praises and helpful guidance. The more that you can accept your true heritage as celestial, as a being spawned by great love, the more willing you will be to accept the benefits that accompany all Children of Love. Your presence in the world makes all beings glad, and we seek to do the same unto you!

Q: How can I discover what my life purpose is?

A: The answer to your question about life purpose is always the same: "love." Yet you may reject this as too simplistic and unspecific. The *form* and *direction* of your life purpose is your actual concern. You truly are asking about your next steps and how to unravel yourself from situations that make you unhappy.

Your in-soul (your higher self) urges you to make each moment meaningful, and we say that this is part of God's plan for you. Use each moment to make another's eyes sparkle and to warm a heart. Use your comforting power to reach out to those in need, and your able hands to relieve stress on Earth's Godly plains. Utilize your talents thus, and you shall be rewarded all your days.

You dream of having greater freedom with respect to time and financial resources so that you may succumb to your deepest wishes. We urge you to indulge in such dreams, and to not regard them as whims. These are the road maps of your life's purpose.

We realize that you ask us this question because you can scarcely believe that these dreams are possibilities. Yet, all who dream and who follow these dreams can testify to you that their success was built upon these same steps of desire, merged with courage and action. You have the same rights as your brethren to accommodate your dreams, Beloved One!

Simplify your desires by accessing them today. Believe that they are at your disposal, and they more readily are. When you pray thus, regarding your life purpose, we answer readily within your heart. We bring to you all of the measures that you could desire. And yet, you stop yourself short by walking away from the dream and toward that which you deem "reality." This needn't be—not any longer, Beloved One.

Put into motion today all of your good intentions. Ease yourself from self-made misery first by adding new dimensions of light into your daily life. Listen to a co-worker, forgive a friend, feed a hungry animal. Any kind act of charity will do. This will give you the impetus to cope with any existing situations that you consider intolerable.

As you add new light into your life, your heart will swell with new-found courage. Use this courage wisely to incorporate more and more steps that remind you of your dream's desires. One on top of the other, these steps succumb in reaching the peak of the mountain surefootedly—until one day you are in the position of answering to others the very question you once asked: "What is my life purpose?" You then reach out your hand, and by example, you show the route to joy, meaning, and fulfillment through the heart's path of desire.

⁓

Q: How can I feel happier?

A: Clearly, this question is in regard to breaking the spell cast over human behavior, which causes you to seek out and find misery. For happiness is your natural state of being, as is true health. Your quest for happiness is actually a desire for wholeness. Since you already have that which you desire, there is no need for outward motion. There is nothing to seek.

The misery habit is satiated the moment that you see greater light within a better alternative. You cannot break away from misery by studying its components. To do so brings you into its mire even more! Holy One, your answers lay before you even now. *Be* happy that you already *are* happy, and it is so.

It is true that certain accoutrements can lend to so-called happiness, yet this form of happiness is short-lived, for thrusting the power of happiness upon outward situations is a sure route to greater misery. Like a thirsty man walking in the desert, perpetually fooled by illusions of water, you who seek happiness through other people need first look within your Holy Self. There shall you find it in buckets.

While it is true that relationships and possessions are part and parcel of your human experience, the real truth is in their enjoyment and appreciation. He who is miserable within his own self is rarely healed of this condition by his surroundings. It is, instead, a change of direction within his heart that propels him to accept happiness as his normal condition.

Rarely is a child taught this simple truth. We witness many children's visions of happiness being outwardly directed toward this prize or that.

We assure you that you already *are* happy, and the *enjoyment* of that happiness is the factor that attracts to you that which you seek. Flex this muscle often, and with practice, this element shines in greater quantities. With intent, happiness can be felt within your body and can be increased in size and strength. We are happy to help you with this intent, reminding you often of its importance.

Q: I truly believe that all prayers are heard, but so many times my prayers haven't been answered. I prayed that my loved one would live, but he died anyway. I prayed for a happy marriage, yet I'm now divorced. Why do my prayers go unanswered?

A: All prayers are heard, meaning that God and Heavenly creation receives all cries for help and all questions needing answers. And these prayers *are* answered, in that they all receive instantaneous replies. The replies may come as comfort or guidance, instructions or information, or what you would term a miraculous "Divine intervention." Answered prayer does not always mean that your "wishes" come true, but it does mean that attention is given to you and the situation without delay.

So, praying has many vital and useful applications. It ensures that the invisible realm embarks upon the visible, thus bringing additional blessings to light. All creatures have this remarkable ability to bring about blessings, merely by being present to the awareness of love. Yet, when humans fumble with fears and doubts, our blessings can help you rise above Earthly consciousness and soar Heavenward, where healing is revealed.

So, when you ask whether you are blocked or doing something "wrong," our answer to you is that you cannot be mistaken when engaging in prayer. Whether you are merely mouthing a prayer through repetition, or are fully engaged in a sincere vow or plea, be assured that your prayer is an effective tool in *any* situation!

When it seems that prayers go unanswered, it may be that fears and doubts are simply blocking your understanding of the light within the situation. For, many times your wishes seem to be defied because there is a lack of information that would help you see the great blessings that arise from the current unfoldment of events. Certainly, more blessings come about with the addition of your holy thoughts, cast Heavenward. And yet, we ask you to trust that regardless of the physical outcome, the spiritual outcome of Divine love is always assured!

There can be no other possible outcome than happiness and love, because nothing else *is* possible. And even when your heart aches with sorrow, your mind trembles with insecurity, and your being is heavy with loneliness, know that we will help you untangle these cords. Do not abandon your prayers simply because you believe that your prayers were abandoned by us! You and your wishes are utterly important to God, but many other factors abide: Divine timing, the will of another person involved, and the greater happiness at the end of the unfoldment are among those reasons why your wishes seemed to have been ignored.

If you can but trust God and His handiworkers to give you comfort, aid, and assurance, you will be opening your arms to receiving these gifts. Doubt and self-pity effectively close your arms across your chest, so you are unable to receive.

Dear One, your Heavenly parent seeks to give you the world! Do not chase anything, but instead, ask and be open-armed to receiving. Be watchful for inner reactions that stir you into action, for these knowings are God's voice calling upon you to receive. God is all-powerful, it is true, but He is not blocking you from happiness in any degree. In contrast, God wills more for your happiness than do you! It is but your definition of what would lead to happiness that is denying you. For when you place conditions upon your happiness, you place that joy in a future tense. How much better would you feel, then, if you allowed yourself happiness today, this very minute? Do you not see the many gifts that would follow? And that the more receptive you are to these gifts, the more intensely they will flow unto you?

Be not afraid of happiness, Darling One. There is not one iota in God's consciousness that would will to test you, to pain you, or to deflect you. You are God's greatest creation, and you are equally great in His gaze with all others! Allow us to bestow upon you the tools that are needed, so that you, too, may shower the world with your gifts. And in an endless circle of givingness, you shall experience the delight that comes from being an Earthly angel.

Q: Are there extraterrestrials, and if so, what is their nature (good or evil)?

A: When you ask about extraterrestrials, we assume that you are referring to beings who live on the landscape of other planets. And if this is truly your question, the answer is, "Yes, most definitely." There are infinite life-forms across the galaxies, sprinkled like stars throughout the various lands. Some are life-forms that are seen, and some are those unseen by human eyes and untouched by human hands. These beings, whom you would term "invisible," are merely housed in a dimension apart from your own. Their environs would be harsh to your dense human form, so they are domiciled within a different framework—one that is quite physical on their plane of dimension, yet one that your scientists may term as "nonexistent."

It is a fallacy to focus upon human conditions and project them onto other species of different origins! Time travel is a human concept, apart from creatures and beings who live without the concept of time. The "rate and speed of travel" is another human precept, projected onto those beings whose abilities of travel exceed your own. Do not be judgmental, then, when measuring the advancement of this or that culture. See them with innocence for what they are: the same beings as yourself—inside—housed in different cultures with different levels of abilities.

So, you are now asking whether extraterrestrials live among you on planet Earth? Would it surprise you if we denied this? You may say that we are splitting hairs, but the fact is that if someone lives upon the earth, they are terrestrial to the planet. They are only extraterrestrial if they do *not* live on the planet. Many creations upon the planet have extraterrestrial origins, yourself included. You are from another dimension, and you have a nonphysical origin. You cannot escape this fact no matter how far you distance yourself from realizing this knowledge.

As far as visitors from other dimensions are concerned, they certainly bombard the earth's atmosphere with various missions. We are among them, from the angelic realm, and yes, there are certainly visitors who "drop by" from other dimensions. Many are scientists who are seeking proof of human reality, for you see, there are rumors of your reality existing on other planets. So, many have attempted to prove or disprove your existence through visitations to human Earth. Those who were able to access your dimension with their perceptual abilities concentrated upon studying you and made reports to take home. Others, who were incapable of noticing you due to perceptual limitations on their part, reported back of your nonexistence.

When you talk about "parallel realities," this is what is meant: the different and various dimensions, some of which are physical and some of which are not. Some of the "higher dimensions" are inaccessible to human form, yet through your psychic senses, you can carve out an awareness of these beings. They are benevolent, and yes, you can place your trust in them, for any of the higher dimensions must operate from love or they could not operate at all. Only the lower-ordered beings can live apart from love, and even then, they are severely hampered in their effectiveness, so they are not to be feared.

Q: Dolphins seem to be unearthly, and I wonder what their origin is and if they have a special purpose upon the earth. Can dolphins really help people?

A: We laugh, for you already know the answer to this one, and yet you ask because you can scarcely believe its validity. Is it beyond human reason that these mighty and gentle beings would have their origin from on-high? Why would they come from a different origin than you, yourself? For your race also has celestial origins. Every being whom your eye witnesses has a celestial origin, for Earth offers a harsh and dense environment that is not welcoming to all concerned. The beings who originate from this locale tend to be harsh and dense themselves—not inferior, mind you—but simply reflecting the environment of their origin.

You recognize within the dolphins the kingdom that you come from yourselves. Their lighthearted laughter, their easy gait splashing through the waves, and their gentle souls remind you of your Heavenly home. And truly, that is the promise that the dolphins bring to this planet: that your origin is from beyond the walls of your environs. The dolphins remind you of this, and also of your purpose. That is why you love them so. Their holy reason for being here is to consecrate the planet with much-needed light, infusing all beings upon the planet with a healthy dose of Heaven's light and lightness.

Spend time with the dolphins often in meditation. They bring great energy to this planet at this time, and all who choose may drink from their well, simply by intending. Although you love to be physically present with your dolphin mates, these connections need not be delayed for a physical meeting, for the great dolphins will surrender to your wish to connect with them on-high. They will extend their essence to meet you—at any time and in any way.

Doreen, you are to teach about the dolphins to many people because these beings are more readily accessible to those who rely upon their physical senses of sight and touch than are we angels. Those who need physical validations of their angels' words will reach their hands out to the dolphins and pull back their hands, transformed into believers. The dolphins can move mountains and build faith, and the more people who swim with them, the better. Hear the dolphins' cries, which are calls to our souls asking us to go deeper with them, until we touch the truth within our essence, within our very being. Let the dolphins be your symbol of peace. Let the dolphins be your model of joy.

Q: I often feel sleepy, like I can't get enough rest, even though I sleep eight hours a night and take naps during the day. Why am I tired so often?

A: You, who are weary as a result of your daily routines, have lost the awareness of unique moments. You have stopped noticing butterflies lighting upon flowers, kittens who rub next to your leg, and clouds that form endless shapes. Your concentration on future goals has robbed you of this moment's joyful playfulness. By living in the future, you are unable to tap in to the very resources that fuel your energy now.

Instead, your focus has been that "I will feel better as soon as I . . ." and then you've put conditions on your future happiness and vitality. Why not decide, instead, that you are happy now? Why delay the inevitable? Wouldn't present happiness help you in the relinquishment of this future focus—all the while allowing you to spend time on your major desires . . . and knowing that you are happy already?

You have complicated your life because you believe that many factors are necessary to bring you happiness—someday. If, instead, you allowed yourself the pleasure of simple happiness in this very moment, you could also eliminate unnecessary complications from your life. Through simplicity, you can lighten the grip of your crowded schedule and the weight of too many physical possessions.

Q: I feel trapped at a job that means nothing to me. I really want to make a difference in the world, but I can't afford to quit my job. What can I do to either change jobs, or add more meaning and pleasure to my existing job?

A: Your intention has already created a distance from you and your job, and we will help you steer its course in the direction that you choose. When your heart nudges you to make a change, you have the choice to either heed its calling or to deny it. When you heed your heart's call to change, you first do so by acknowledging your dissatisfaction. This is where prayer comes in—when you ask for assistance in creating change. It is necessary for you to detach from how that change will come about, for the Infinite Wisdom has many courses to choose from, and you wouldn't want to steer it toward one of less satisfaction through an insistence on one certain way. So, make your prayer for meaning and happiness with your work, and then stand back, awaiting inner instructions as to your role. Working in conjunction with Heavenly guides, your changes *will* come about in a monumental way. How could it be otherwise, when there is no stopping the forces of Heaven?

Now, denying your heart's calling is an entirely different matter, and this is where dissatisfaction comes to play. For we tell you that as long as you are flowing along the river of your Divinely guided instructions, your heart will be filled with joy from day one, until the day your change is completely in place.

But if you wallow in hesitation, doubt, or indecision, you thwart the river-flow of Heaven's helpfulness. Focus not upon the dark movie of fear, but go inward where the light always brightly shines. We will fill your heart with courage, peacefulness, and motivation.

When you state that you cannot change a condition because of this reason or that, you have claimed that reality as your own. We cannot interfere with your decision, although we can gently remind you that nothing interferes with Divinely guided change. So, cling not to your illusions of financial traps in this situation, but surrender them instead to God, for God knows no limits in His kingdom!

As you make your changes, they will go as quickly as you feel comfortable. You can always slow the flow, as you feel it necessary. Should you desire an instant change, that is certainly available to you, as your heart desires.

During this time of transition, it is important for your well-being to focus on the changeless within you and the situation. Blame not these circumstances upon another person, but always see the unchanging truth of each and every being—yourself included—of Divine Light and Love. See the inner joy within everyone, regardless of the surface conditions that appear. As you see the holiness within each one, you more readily see this Divinity within your own self. This elevated stance of everyone helps you to reach much higher than you ever have before so that you can be comfortable in your new situation. Otherwise, a diminished view of yourself as "less than" will cause you to stir with new rumbles of dissatisfaction once you reach your new destination.

Let the healing, then, be both within and without. Let the changelessness of your God-state reach your full awareness so that you can capture its essence in your physical plane.

Q: I've been alone for a long, long time without a real relationship. I keep praying for a soulmate to come into my life, but I haven't even had a date for a year! What is blocking me?

A: We seek to help those who are lonely and afraid. Your fear that you will be alone forever is your greatest barrier to reaching your intended destination of matrimony. You are pushing away that desire through your actions, which stem from fear of loneliness. You fear, ultimately, that you are unlovable, and this fear diminishes the intensity at which you shine. Attract your Beloved One with your sure knowingness of your Godly nature. *Know* that you are God's lovely child! This is the knowingness that attracts to you all that you desire and so much more.

You believe that your fears of unworthiness are hidden, but they are actually on display for all the world to see. These fears send a signal that is traceable to the many events that have reinforced this fear. Do you see, then, that your question about whether or not you are lovable attracts answers from the universe to support your vision of yourself? Decide again, and see a new set of experiences impart themselves to you. The world will reinforce the degree of attractiveness that you believe you possess. It's all in the belief. Believe us on this count, Dear One. You *are* wholly lovable, yet until you believe it yourself, you shall not witness its truth.

Q: How can I know if my current love partner is my soulmate?

A: We hear this question again and again, and we know that the root question is: "Is there someone else with whom I could be happier and better suited?" To ask whether this person is your soulmate is irrelevant to the true, underlying question, for even a soulmate who is from your soul-group pod in Heaven is not enough to assure you of the happiness that you seek.

Compatibility shifts with changing interests and priorities, which are bound to shift within any given partnership. It is impossible for two partners to share identical skills and interests, yet their differences can still result in "sharings" that create a climate of compatibility. The key component is trust for one another. With trust, the rest falls easily into place. Trust builds and grows as each shows honor to the other. And trust ensures that your love bond will grow.

With trust, you feel free to share with one another the contents of your heart. You can rest easy, knowing that your sharing is received with openness and respect. Without trust, there is a momentary hesitation, where the safety of sharing with the other is questioned. Do you want to build a greater bond of trust within your partnership? Then begin sharing with your partner the contents of your heart: your dreams and desires. Then, listen in return as your partner shares with you.

Listen quietly and patiently to one another, without criticism or contempt of any form. For so often, partners throw their own fears up as barriers against truly hearing their partners' concerns and dreams. They listen to their partner, thinking only, *Well, how does this affect me?* When you listen from the perspective of quiet listening, however, you will see your partner's plans unfold in harmony with you. If they do not unfold harmoniously with your own, that can be one signal that the purpose of the partnership is over.

Similarly, if you find that your partnership does not warrant your trust as a result of betrayal and criticism, you must attempt to teach your partner the importance of these relationship components without delay. If your partner resists your attempts at these teachings—and if you are very sure that you are offering these teachings with honor, trust, and gentle love—then you may have to consider that your partnership is beyond repair. At that point, reach Heavenward, and ask your in-soul (higher self) and us angels for our guidance. We, you can trust. We are wholly worthy of your trust if you are willing to trust *your* feelings on this account. Some of you have become so detached from your inner mechanism that you do not know what trust truly feels like. So, allow us to teach you these steps to regain faith and trust, Dear One. We will gently guide you home, for your soul is inherently trusting, and it is your soul that we seek to reveal to you.

Q: I'm thinking about going into business for myself, but I'm not sure if it's the right thing to do. How can I know if self-employment would be right for me or not?

A: You dream of self-employment as an avenue of escape and freedom, and in many ways, you would realize these qualities. Yet, your dream must be tempered with the realization that, if you jump headlong into self-employment without tempering your enthusiasm with a healthy dose of realism, your dreams can be dashed before they have the chance to bloom. You need a rest and an escape, that is certain. And you *can* carve out a period of rest in which you can explore your options without stress or strain. This step you must take, without delay. For only a clear mind can clearly receive guidance for such an important venture.

It is true that, no matter the outcome of your business decision, you will gain valuable experiences and insights. Everything that you do has the potential to support you, both financially and emotionally. Yet, we caution you against running headfirst into self-employment without a period of rest initially to cool your heels, and to gain new insights and understandings.

This we can tell you: Be very honest with yourself about all the aspects you are considering. Think not only about the money you shall gain, or the opportunities for freedom, for such a focus can lead you to dead ends and further entrapment in the form of debts and legalities. Concentrate, instead, on giving service in a way that brings you great pleasure and enjoyment. Through giving service, you are fed in many ways. First, you receive others' blessings and gratitude—and do not overlook the power that comes from being a beneficiary to these two forces. Second, you are feeding the universe through your service—and the universe *must* feed you in return. Given the universe's great expanse of power and size, you are most likely the recipient who will benefit more in this exchange. Third, by surrounding yourself with enjoyable activities, your inner fuel is maintained by enthusiasm and excitement.

We see many of you open a business and then gleefully wait for customers to arrive. When you encounter delays and frustrations, you begin to doubt your dream. We watch many business owners develop auras of negativity, and they are quite relieved when their businesses later close. These closures should not be pitied, but understood as a decision that the owner was tired of the business and wished that it would go away. The only businesses that thrive are those in which the owner is filled with joy and excitement at their occupation. Those who feel this gladness send love waves that entice customers to return again and again. To maintain such zeal, though, requires a business owner to "stay in the moment," as you say, to reevaluate present business plans constantly, and to capitalize upon the heart's desires and creative insights.

Do not delay in giving service, awaiting the day when you leave your present job, for many opportunities to give joyfully await you today. Merely hold the thought in mind that you would like to find these opportunities, and the world will rush to present them to you. And you shall taste the sweet nectar of this flow of giving and receiving.

In the ultimate sense, you *are* self-employed presently, for you make the choice of what your employment options are. Your decision to work for others still comes from you, making you the boss of your own ways and schedule. You are the force that drives you to seek employment for money or for meaning—it's *your* choice.

Q: Why do I have a constant sense of time urgency?

A: Your inner awareness tells you that you are not engaged fully in your life's mission, and it sends signals to elicit your attention. Although your soul exists in a timeless universe, it is also programmed to complete this mission within your lifetime. It thus operates within the confines of time, while performing tasks that defy Earthly time-space rules. That is because the soul is not governed by Earthly directives. Only the body complies with these measures. And while the body has elected for a finite destiny upon Earthly time, the soul urges the body to take actions that will fulfill the soul's mission and bring the benefits of joy to the body.

In your solar plexus, which is near the stomach region, you often experience a sense of tightness and dread. There is a pushing and pulling sensation in which you are urged to move forward and make significant contributions to Earth, and another powerful sensation that urges you toward complacency and doubt. The forward push is from your soul, and the fearful pull is from your ego. Both seem to battle for your schedule, yet the soul's voice calls to you so deeply as to never be ignored.

You, who delay your soul's signals to grow, give, teach, and heal, cannot smother its beautiful voice. You can merely ignore it on a conscious level. Yet, still your inner wisdom hears the soul's urgings very loud and very clear.

Instead of praying for more time in your schedule, it is wiser to pray for help with the fears that fuel your ego's dictates. Call upon us angels to amplify your soul's sweet voice, and leap with joy in union with its directives. *Your soul will keep you safe* and give you the clear and loving guidance you seek. It will accompany you out of the traps in which you feel mired.

Q: I feel like I'm blocked in some way. Can you tell me what my block is and how to remove it?

A: Dear One, this question comes from a feeling that some dark force is imposing its will upon your own. And in the case of certain blocks, they are merely your fears of moving forward into lightness. The fear of happiness is rampant among many humans, and it comes from a deep distrust of that which you have rarely known. The unfamiliar is often frightening, for fear of what it might bring. And so you cling tightly to the familiar, even if it is a source of continual pain.

When you seek to hear the Divine voice, or to commune visually with Spirit, and cannot hear and cannot see, it is merely because of your shyness, which shrinks in the face of greatness. Beloved One, you are great, mighty, and powerful, also! Be not afraid of your own greatness, but allow us to mirror it for you during our communications. For, as you witness our greatness visually and with naked ears fully opened to love's voice, there you will witness your own Divinity.

Do you not see, then, that a block is merely another way to say that you are fearful of seeing your holy self in the mirror? You guard against fright of what you might see, imagining that your own reflection will be that of a hideous monster. And so you delay witnessing this reflection, blaming the situation upon some unknown "block."

A block is not a reality unless you focus upon it in a constant state of awareness. When you nurture your block by constantly affirming its presence, you give it reality, scope, and size! So, right this very moment, gaze away from the block's seeming presence. See it in a new light, as merely a stepping-stone that will cause you to learn of others' fears and doubts so that you might have increased compassion for a brother or sister who suffers in the same way.

Decide upon your greatness, knowing that you share this with all the world. You, who are aware of your Divinity, are obligated to awaken this awareness within others. By God's hand, we will bring others to your side who thirst for this Divine quenching. You will teach others about their own greatness, and your adventures in doing so will be many and varied. Enjoy them all for their richness of experience. Soak them up, and replenish yourself frequently at our well.

Q: How can I know when a relationship is over and it's time to move on?

A: Staleness settles into any relationship where communication has become devoid of truth and freshness. Think about a relationship when it is young and new: You share your heart's contents and exclaim in exuberance, "Me, too!" You seek for similarities with your new beloved, and you delight when you find similarities in your midst.

Staleness emanates from a relationship when your focus turns to finding differences that distinguish you from your mate. Distrust causes you to hesitate in sharing the contents of your heart with one another. And as you pull back your candid nature, so too do you also pull back your energy from one another. The retreated energy disconnects you from each other.

Sometimes, then, a stale relationship can be revived by entering into another process similar to a new partnership, wherein you share the contents of your heart with naive exposure to one another. This approach, where you remove caution and ramble about your hopes, your dreams, and your aspirations—without receiving criticism from your partner—can heal a relationship that is sick or dying. It is certainly worth an attempt in this direction, to see if your partnership can be revived.

Each relationship has, at its heart, a holy purpose. Sometimes this purpose involves teaching us a personal lesson, such as patience or understanding. Sometimes the relationship helps us with our life's purpose. We never become involved with someone accidentally. Even "casual" relationships come with a purpose for us to learn and share in. We feel the most excitement when we recognize that we are with a new person with whom we share a sense of connection. This connection or attraction is a signal that there is a purpose in your joining. As long as the partnership serves this purpose, you will feel the attraction. When the purpose has been served, the attraction will cease. At that point, you must make the choice as to whether to end the relationship, to slow it down, or to continue the relationship from a new perspective.

Regardless, you will know that you spent time in the relationship with a holy master, just as you are one. Each person with whom you spend even the smallest amount of time is the same as the person with whom you spend eternity. No one has lesser or greater importance in the drama of your life span. All bring gifts to share, which they place at your feet at the conclusion of your relationship. Your gratitude toward the brothers and sisters with whom you have shared moments is appropriate.

So, how do you know if a relationship is over? You will know this if you have been unhappy for some length of time and have attempted to communicate this discontent to your partner without success. If you have felt dissatisfied, no longer feel attracted to your partner, and the pull to be together is completely gone, then it may be time to move on. You would not want to prevent your partner, or yourself, from encountering the next person who brings an essential piece of the puzzle into your lives. You will help each other by discussing your options—including the possible parting of ways—so that you can create a vacuum that nature can fill with your new relationships.

Q: What do the angels say about homosexuality?

A: This question pertains to the question of what is right and wrong, and we shall focus instead upon—as you humans put it—"inalienable rights." These include your right to choose and make decisions free of barriers and restrictions. More than a right, this is a need to overcome barriers and be limitless and free. This is as true with your speech as it is with the nature of your sexual orientation.

The human origin began when human beings first seeded the idea of conscious independence into their mind-field. This sparked the origination of the idea of planets and locales where they would be free to explore their conscious universe. When humans first landed upon this great planet, they were not accustomed to taking control over their lives to such a degree. So, they built in certain dependencies that were of their own invention. And thus, they restricted themselves with regulations and rules. These were created due to humans' inherent distrust of their own inner guidance system.

The bodies that you possess are part of this massively contained experiment, in which humans seek to counter their independence with the mastery of their free will. As such, they inadvertently restrict themselves by pouring their soul into a container, which is the body, and then running about with focus on maintaining that body. Such exertion is a distraction from the central point of the essence of one's being, the mighty love within.

You, who *are* love Divine, cannot withstand a steady focus away from the awareness of love. Yet, when confusion reigns over the source of your emptiness, you seek to fulfill it with the body. Thus, you turn to needs of the appetite to fulfill yourself. However, the body's satiation is always temporary, while the soul's is always assured and eternal.

That is why we do not involve ourselves directly in the nature of your sexuality and other appetites, except to the degree that they distract your attention from the Divine love that eternally resides within you and all beings. When your appetite creates barriers for love's gate, there will we intervene, first with gentle reminders about the nature of happiness, then with more specific reminders about your Heavenly home. Shame and guilt are not in our vocabulary, yet your own ego haunts you with these unloving conditions. You, who are entirely built upon a foundation of love, though, could hardly withstand anything that is unloving for too long.

The nature of your sexual orientation, therefore, is the least of our concerns. Our central message to you is essential to your present level of happiness: You are already a Divine being of God. No improvement is needed or necessary to achieve that state. No one and no thing can eradicate your holy inheritance as God's sons and daughters. What you make of your *awareness* of your existence, however, is entirely of your own choosing. You do have the right to create any level of existence that you desire—whether it is one of persecution, shame, or guilt; or whether it is an existence of service and devotion to the Light within. Our role is essentially to stand before you and behind you, sheltering you from self-made storms should you call for our help. We could never cease to love you, not now or ever. Built out of, and upon, Divine love, we are clear in our knowledge of who we are in relationship to your holy selves: one with our infinite Creator, Who is God eternal.

Q: How do I know if I should move to a new location?

A: When you feel the urge to transform your living environment, several factors must be considered. First of all, consider whether this is truly your in-soul (higher self) urging you to move. If it is Divinely directed, your in-soul will ensure that you get the message clearly. You will come across many references that point the way to your move. You will have a haunting urge that is undying. And yet, the opposite can also be true, when your ego takes this form in its continual effort to place happiness in some future locale. Your ego, you see, tries to convince you that moving is in your best interests, when it will really create upheavals in many areas of your life. Being uprooted robs you of many precious resources, and it takes a good measurement of Earthly time to recover. Yet, in some instances, such a move is truly the embodiment of "out with the old and in with the new."

Your assignment, then, is to capture that voice that elects for your move and study it closely. Is it urging you to move to escape? That is the ego's calling. Or, is it calling you to move to bring you closer to God? That is your in-soul being Divinely directed. Consider marginal alternatives to a move, including sprucing up your living environment to create a sense of newness. Ask experts to come in and advise you on the best ways to make your present living situation more accommodating and palatable.

When you are Divinely directed to move, you will not question the decision, for the urging will be so strong and so lovingly positioned in your mind that not a single doubt can be harbored there. When it is Divinely guided for you to move, you will know with great certainty that your presence is *needed* in another community. You will be *drawn* to your new locale, rather than feeling that you are *escaping* from your present conditions. Only through this attraction will you truly know your rightful home. Do not seek to force or push such a move, for it will only mean another temporary transition for you. Pray, wait, and listen for our guidance, which we will bring to you on Heaven's wings.

We *will* help you to accommodate your present living conditions to bring you Earthly peace, comfort, and happiness. We will help you to know when the time is right to move, and to which location. Until you reach such certainty, we urge you to grow in peace in your present living situation. Carry on, awaiting your in-soul's firm decision to move. If you will patiently wait, we promise you a smooth and harmonious move, with all of the doors opening in succession for you.

Q: What happens when someone commits suicide?

A: When souls seek to obliterate pain by the taking of their body's life-force, they are guided by their ego to escape. The ultimate in escape mechanisms is to attempt to run away from the Earth plane by ceasing to be. This plan never works, for as you know, the consciousness never dies, even when the body's breathing mechanisms come to a halt.

Souls then arrive in consciousness in a higher state of awareness once the body is removed. Their pain is eased by our presence, yet it is reinflicted whenever the soul witnesses the sorrow of their Earth family and the pain that their actions have engendered upon them. The soul sheds tears alongside your own, and suffers from the deepest of regrets. This sorrow is the essence of your tale of a hell-like situation in which those who commit suicide are cast.

It is not true that these souls are punished or judged in any way, but many who commit this act do punish and judge their own selves quite harshly. And for that, they do indeed suffer! You, who survive these beings, can help the most by laying aside your anger, fear, and guilt about the situation, and focusing solely upon love and empathy for all.

Make it your gift to each other to uplift the persons involved by surrounding them in an aura of the whitest of light. See them floating on a billowy cloud of compassion. Worry not about your loved one's safety or comfort, and wallow not in your thoughts of what might have been. Let blame be replaced by understanding, and allow love to heal all wounds.

Each time a soul commits suicide, additional angels are sent to the family's side, for Heaven has great understanding of the difficulties that an Earthly incarnation involves. And for those who seek escape, options other than suicide are certainly available. Yet, there are those who are unaware of these options, and who see suicide as their only route to escape. Have compassion for their decision, Beloved Ones, and know that these are individuals who are learning, just as you are. Although you may call their actions "selfish" in many respects, these souls were seeking to help you by removing themselves from your sphere. For those who commit suicide feel completely unlovable, unworthy of their family's attention. These souls seek to completely remove themselves, and once the decision has been made, they will rarely seek a solution other than the one their mind has set forth.

Then they take their body's life, sometimes in a rash way, other times in a meticulously planned way. It is not for us to decide what is right or wrong, once the damage has been incurred. It is only our responsibility to heal the situation through prayer, Divine love, and understanding.

Know that your loved ones are being taken care of—whether they are in the physical plane or among us in the spirit world. Our wings wrap around them and grip them with the mighty force that helps them to feel safe and loved. We shall not let go of your loved ones, nor of you. No matter what physical actions a human may make, our love goes on without condition or judgment. We know that death is not final, and that pain is unreal in the face of love. Once in heaven, your departed loved ones realize the extent of how deeply you did, and still do, love them.

And in the most seemingly painful of situations, we send you additional doses of love's light. Be gentle with yourselves, Dearest Ones, and know that you live close to God's heart.

Q: *Is life really based on free will, or is everything predestined?*

A: Free will is left to your discretion as to whether or not to follow the path that is ascribed to you. Yes, there is free will, most certainly. And yet, sometimes you choose not to see life in that way. And that choice of *viewpoint* is a freewill choice! Protecting yourself behind an armor of "victimhood," you pretend that your careless choices were causeless as far as you were concerned. In that way, you cease to feel the stinging arrow of the wound that bleeds from decisions that you made. Once again, an outer focus takes away the power to disrupt these wrong-minded choices. Only an inner focus is needed to interrupt a situation that gallops away from the direction of love.

There are no "bad guys" in your midst, only bad choices. This is not to say that there are absolute rights or wrongs, for who among us could judge such causality? Yet there are choices for love and those for fear. And the latter shall always create misery, while the former shall always keep peace in conscious awareness.

Do you see, then, why it is a bad choice to believe that there are others in your midst who are responsible for your wrong choices? Such a viewpoint stems from many fears, and thus lends itself to misery and dejection. For why should you even try if you are but a victim of outward circumstances and cruel people?

Consider, instead, taking a vantage point of total freedom. You, who have such power that it is unequaled by any other, could no more be powerless than could God. Your will has never separated from the Creator, and thus, it is fully aligned with His own. We, who are assigned to watch over your care, come directly from the same Great Mind that is within each one of us. There has never been a separation, nor can one ever exist.

"The Law of Free Will," of which you speak often, is nothing more than a "theme," rather than a law. The word *law* implies that it can be broken. Yet, this is never the case. Free will can never be hampered or broken, because it is the very nature of how we were created. Nothing that is created can be undone.

The process of wielding meaning from each sentence that you read involves your free will, for instance, for you are free to interpret our words in myriad ways. We beseech you to follow love within your heart, and to maintain an inward focus, but that is all. We cannot tie your hands and force you to be of service to your fellow human beings. Yet, we can interrupt a flow based upon fearful thinking with a reminder that peacefulness lies in another direction.

The plan that God has for us isn't really a plan at all; it is a prescribed reality to which no alternative lies. The bliss of our Creator forever permeates all of creation, and it is only in the forgetting that misery exists. You are already in the midst of this blissful reality, and you needn't seek for it a moment longer.

So, do you see that your question is answered by a twofold explanation? God's will and bliss are fixed without possibility of change. And your free will exists simply in your ability to choose between this bliss or a different reality of your own making. We are simply along with you in case you choose the latter. For, in God's bliss, no angels are needed to rescue you from fear! No problems exist that need erasure, and there is no lack. For what but that which reflects a mortal's fears could need our assistance? In God's perfect kingdom, you are without need of any kind.

Q: How do I know if my deceased loved ones are okay?

A: Your worries about your loved ones are primarily a projection of your guilt. You are concerned that you have erred in the past and that your loved ones harbor grudges against you. You fret that your loved ones suffered during their demise, and you question whether they cease to be.

The death of loved ones is surely a crushing blow to the survivors, but not to the departed souls, who cross the barriers of the threshold of pain and suffering. No more do they wonder about their identity, for they are surrounded by Heavenly beings who remind them of their God-given loveliness. No more do they worry about their future, for they live in the eternal now. And yet if they did suffer during Earthly hardship, they are fully freed of it now. They cast off the memory of those hardships and ask that you do the same on their behalf.

Do not worry that you fell short of some self-perceived mark in bringing comfort to your loved ones' lives when they were living! Do not imagine that you are to blame for their suffering or their death! For each has their own mark, when they must return home to their Heavenly Creator's waiting arms. Each has a Divinely inspired appointment to traverse the veil toward the Heavenly home. In that home, no harsh words are exchanged, so there is no room for regret or harsh judgment. Surrounded by the glory of love, your departed ones live on in a cushion of bliss. They have no time to count others' misdeeds. They are amassing an inventory of their own actions during their Earthly life. They see their misdirections, and they are counseled by angels to not be harsh with self-judgment, but merely to learn from their mistakes and move on. Heaven wills the same for all of creation, including yourself.

So, you see, Beloved One, no one in Heaven holds grudges against you for your perceived lapses. No one in Heaven holds on to their suffering without extraordinary effort. Heaven simply will not support the outlook of the ego, and your loved ones in Heaven shine their love upon you now. Worry not about your loved ones, Holy Child of God, but instead, place your efforts into your own noble life of service. Build your awareness of God's holy grace, and focus not on fantasies of pain. Your prayers on your loved ones' behalf are transmitted directly, and they are the greatest gift that you give—not only to your loved ones, but most certainly to your own self.

Editor's note: *This concludes the channeled portion of the book. Everything that follows is in Doreen Virtue's voice.*

PART V

Communing with
Your Angels

Who the Angels Are

The word *angel* means "messenger." Angels bring messages from the Divine Mind of our Creator. They are gifts to us from God, sent to us to help us remember our Divine nature, to be loving and kind, to discover and polish our talents for the betterment of the world, and to keep us from harm's way before our time. They also guide us in areas of relationships, health, career, and even finances.

Your angels are with you to enact God's plan of peace. They help you to be peaceful, because one person at a time, a world of peaceful people equals a peaceful world. That's why your angels desire to help you in any way that will lead you to peace. You aren't bothering them or wasting their time if you ask for "small" favors. The angels know that minor irritants often add up to major stress, so it's their great pleasure to help you with anything standing in your way.

Now while it's true that challenges do make us grow, the angels also say that peace leads to even bigger growth spurts. Through peace, our schedules and creativity are more open to giving service. Through peace, our bodies operate in a healthy fashion. Through peace, our relationships thrive and blossom. Through peace, we are shining examples of God's love.

Every once in a while, I'll receive a letter from someone accusing me of worshiping angels. The letter writer emphasizes that we're only supposed to worship *God.*

I always reply in the same way: with love. We all make the mistake of assuming something about a person without checking the facts. Anyone who has read one of my books, listened to one of my audiotapes, or attended one of my workshops realizes that I emphasize that all glory *does* go to God. The angels certainly don't want to be worshiped. And I absolutely never suggest that we should worship them.

That being said, here's a gentle reminder: God is everywhere. God is within you. God is within me. And God is definitely within all of the angels. So, we do give glory to God *within all of us* when we give glory to God.

Some of my audience members who have a hard time with organized religion don't want to hear this. Perhaps a woman's father abused her, so she rejects all father figures—even God. (Of course, God is an androgynous force Who is both our spiritual Mother *and* Father.) Or maybe some member of an organized religion did a man harm, so he rejects anything smacking of religion, even his spirit guides and angels. Or it could be that religion is just illogical to another person, so she stops thinking about anything spiritual. Perhaps someone else feels guilty because of his lifestyle, and deep down, he fears that God may "punish" him, so he tries to block out all awareness of God. Or, maybe a woman fears that God will try to control her and push her into a lifestyle devoid of fun.

Some people ask me whether it's "okay" to speak directly to God or to the angels, or whether this is blasphemous. I certainly prescribe that we follow our personal beliefs when talking to Heaven. However, if God, the ascended masters, and the angels are truly one, then why would it be "wrong" to talk directly to the angels? Aren't you merely accepting a gift that God has bestowed upon you? You and your angels aren't conspiring against God in some sort of mutinous plot. The angels (as well as your higher self) will never defy God's will, so there's no fear that you might make a mistake.

The angels are aware of your "dream of fear," as well as the truth of Divine love. God, being All-Love, has no awareness of anything *but* love.

God can tell when your consciousness is shut away from Him, and that you're having a nightmare, but He cannot tell what the nightmare's about. That would require Him to be less than 100 percent love. The angels are a bridge between the truth and your nightmarish illusion of problems. They can help bring you back from your nightmares into your happy waking state of health, happiness, peace, and abundance. They work in conjunction with your higher self, and any ascended master you are spiritually aligned with, such as Jesus, Moses, Quan Yin, the Holy Spirit, Buddha, Yogananda, or whomever. The angels don't judge your beliefs. They realize that if they tried to change those opinions, you wouldn't listen to them anyway. Rather, the angels work within your present beliefs as a way to reach you.

The *Course in Miracles* says that God doesn't help us out during times of trouble because He sees no need (seeing only love and perfection, not the illusion of lack or problems), but He does send helpers when we think we're in trouble. It's not that God ignores us; it's just that God's way of helping is to know that everything already is fixed in truth. But just in case we insist on staying asleep to that truth, God created angels to help us find our way out of the nightmares we create.

The angels have told me that we wouldn't need them if we stayed fully aware of love's presence at all times. Since we channel-surf between varying degrees of fear and love, however, God sends us angels to help us out.

When It's a Person's Time to Go

In my work as a clairvoyant medium who converses with the deceased, and as a researcher who has reviewed hundreds of cases of near-death experiences, I'm convinced that we can't die unless it's our time to go. We can mess up our lives or our bodies, and we can have close calls, but unless it's our "time," death cannot ring our doorbell.

Each of us creates a basic life plan prior to incarnation. This plan includes the form your life purpose will take (such as writer, healer, musician, teacher, and so on). The plan also includes some of the major experiences and relationships you'll encounter. This isn't a fatalistic philosophy. We each choose these experiences prior to coming to Earth—our free will is entirely involved. Plus, we don't plan our whole lives ahead of time. Instead, we only devise the major intersections and some overall themes, such as the personal lessons we'll learn during our incarnation (patience or compassion, for instance).

We also come up with two, three, or more ages when we will exit the physical plane and return to our Heavenly home—for instance, ages 18, 47, and 89. Each time one of these ages comes up for you, you'll have an intersection occur (such as an accident, disease, or suicidal thought) which will give you the option of going to Heaven or staying on Earth. Most people opt for longer lives so that they can be with their Earthly families for a generation or two. But some people plan early exits, and they return home before their bodies reach full maturity on Earth. Even though their bodies were small, though, their souls may have been older than yours or mine when they left the Earth plane.

Your higher self knows the different ages when you contracted to leave the Earth plane—and you can discover what they are by simply asking your higher self, "What age will I be when I leave this physical body?" Most of you will automatically hear (with your inner ear) three ages. Some of you will see numbers in front of you. Still others will receive nothing—usually because you subconsciously don't want to know the answer. There are some who will hear an age that is just around the corner, and then hear nothing else. This can mean that your time is almost up, or that your ego is running rampant, trying to scare you. After all, the ego operates from fear. Ninety-nine percent of the time, you have older ages coming up, but your fear is preventing you from hearing those numbers. Relaxation, breath, and meditation can help you hear the answers accurately.

The committee that helps you draw up this plan includes the beings who will stay by your side as your guardian angels and spirit guides. You each have at least two guardian angels, from start to finish. Everyone also has at least one spirit guide, and usually more. Guardian angels are those beings who haven't incarnated as humans (unless they were *incarnated* angels, a topic beyond the scope of this book, but is covered in my books *Healing with the Angels* and *Healing with the Fairies*). Your spirit guides are usually your deceased loved ones. When you're young, they consist of relatives who passed away before you were born.

These guides and angels help keep you on-track in fulfilling your life's purpose and learning your personal lessons. They also help you avoid messing up your lives or bodies. They intervene, without needing your permission, if you're about to be killed before it's your time to die. If one of your "intersection" ages comes up, where you could opt out and die, the angels and guides assist you with your decision making. Usually, if a person hasn't yet fulfilled their life's purpose and learned their personal lessons, and especially if a person has living loved ones, that individual will choose to stick around until their next intersection age comes up.

I learned firsthand that the angels can only help us to the degree to which we'll allow them. In 1995, a loud and clear male angel's voice warned me that unless I put the top up on my convertible car, it would be stolen. For varying reasons, I didn't follow the angel's guidance, and I ended up in an armed carjacking one hour later. Then the angel told me to scream with all my might. This time I listened, and my screams attracted the attention of passersby who came to my rescue.

I had the choice, both times when the angel attempted to help me, to listen or to ignore him. If I had ignored his second warning to "scream with all your might," then I don't know if I would still be alive today. But I do know this: If I had died, at least I would know that the angels did their best to intervene and prevent my death. I've seen this same type of freewill choice in everyone I've spoken to—both those who have had a brush with death, and those who have succumbed and who have spoken to me from the Other Side.

Guardian Angels

Guardian angels are personally assigned to you for your entire life. Again, these angels have never lived as humans on Earth unless they were "incarnated angels" (angels who take human form, either briefly or for a lifetime).

As I mentioned earlier, every single person, regardless of faith, character, or lifestyle, has at least two guardian angels (whether that person listens to their angels, though, is an entirely different matter). One guardian angel is your extroverted "nudging" angel, who pushes you to make choices in keeping with your highest self. This angel knows your talents and potential and encourages you to shine brightly in all ways.

The other guardian angel is much quieter in its voice and energy level. This angel comforts you when you're sad, lonely, or disappointed. She hugs you when you don't get the job or apartment you desperately wanted, and calms you when your Friday-night date doesn't show up.

You can have more than two guardian angels—in fact, most people I meet have many more than two. However, my sampling comes from people who attend my workshops, and generally, those who appreciate angels usually attract *more* angels. It's not that angels are biased in favor of their fans; it's just that those who are angelically inclined tend to ask for additional angels. This request is always fulfilled, no matter who asks.

Our angels *do* have gender energies that make them distinctively look and act male or female. However, each of us has angels with different ratios of male to female. So you might have three male angels and one female angel, while your sister has two female angels.

All angels really do have wings and an angelic appearance, similar to the Renaissance paintings depicted on holiday cards and religious paintings. They don't use these wings for transportation in my experience, as I've never seen an angel flap its wings. I've seen them enfold a person in their wings for comfort, and that's the only purpose that the wings have, from what I've witnessed. One time, the angels told me that the only reason they have wings is due to our Western expectations. They said, *"The original painters of angels mistook our aura of light for wings, so they depicted us with wings in their paintings, and we appear to you this way so that you will know that it is us, your angels."*

Interestingly, the guardian angels surrounding people of Eastern religious orientations, such as those who practice Buddhism or Hinduism, usually don't have wings. Their angels are akin to *Bodhisattvas* (enlightened sentient beings), performing the same role as the Western guardian angels: to love, protect, and guide the person to whom they're assigned. The only exceptions are those Easterners who come from eclectic or New Age backgrounds. In those cases, these individuals have large groups of spiritual helpers around them. Typically, such a person will tell me, "I called upon *everyone* in Heaven to surround and help me!"

The Archangels

The archangels oversee the guardian angels. They are usually larger, stronger, and more powerful than the angels. Depending upon your belief system, there are four, seven, or an infinite number of archangels. In this book, Archangel Uriel said that we would meet additional archangels in the near future, almost like discovering new planets or solar systems.

The archangels are nondenominational, and they help anyone, regardless of their religious or nonreligious background. They are able to be with each one of us, individually and simultaneously, because they are beyond space-and-time restrictions. Imagine what your life would be like if you could be in many different places at the same time! Well, the angels say that the only reason we don't experience bilocality is because we *believe* that we can only be in one place at a time. Soon, we'll learn how to lift that restriction, according to the angels.

The reason why I emphasize this point is that some people worry that if they call upon Archangel Michael, for example, they might be pulling him away from a more "important" assignment. This is how we project our human limitations upon the archangels! The fact is that the archangels and the ascended masters can be with anyone who calls upon them, and have a completely unique experience with each being. So know that you can call upon the archangels by mentally asking them to help you. No formal prayers are necessary.

The exact number of archangels who exist depends upon which belief system or spiritual text you consult. The Bible, the Koran, the Testament of Levi, the Kabbalah, the Third Book of Enoch, and the writings of Dionysius all list and describe differing numbers and names of archangels.

There are many archangels, although I usually only highlight Michael, Raphael, Uriel, and Gabriel in my books and workshops. However, the other archangels have lately been urging me to involve them in my life and work. Here are some descriptions of archangels, and how you may wish to work with them:

— **Archangel Ariel's** name means "lion or lioness of God." Ariel is known as the Archangel of the Earth because she works tirelessly on behalf of the planets. Ariel oversees the elemental kingdom, and helps in the healing of animals, especially the nondomesticated kind. Call upon Ariel to become better acquainted with the fairies, to help with environmental concerns, or to heal an injured wild bird or animal.

— **Archangel Azrael's** name means "whom God helps." Azrael is sometimes called the "Angel of Death" because he meets people at the time of their physical death and escorts them to the other side. He helps newly crossed-over souls to feel comfortable and very loved. Azrael helps ministers of all religions, and also spiritual teachers. Call upon Azrael for your deceased or dying loved ones, and also for help with your formal or informal ministry.

— **Archangel Chamuel's** name means "he who sees God." This archangel is also known by several other names, including Camael, Camiel, Camiul, Camniel, Cancel, Jahoel, Kemuel, Khamael, Seraphiel, and Shemuel. Archangel Chamuel helps us find and locate important parts of our lives. Call upon Chamuel to find a new love relationship, new friends, a new job, or any lost item. Once found, Chamuel will help you build and maintain your new situation. So, call upon Chamuel if you need help in repairing any misunderstandings in any personal or work relationship.

— **Archangel Gabriel's** name means "God is my strength." In early Renaissance paintings and ancient writings, Gabriel is portrayed as a female archangel, although later writings refer to Gabriel in masculine pronouns (perhaps because of the Constantine Council's massive editing of scriptures). She is the messenger angel who helps all Earth messengers, such as writers, teachers, and journalists. Call upon Gabriel to overcome fear or procrastination in any endeavor involving communication.

— **Archangel Haniel's** name means "grace of God." Call upon Haniel whenever you wish to add grace and its effects (peace, serenity, enjoyment of good friends' company, beauty, harmony, and so on) to your life. You can also call upon Haniel before any event in which you desire to be the embodiment of grace, such as giving an important presentation, being interviewed for a job, or going on a first date, for instance.

— **Archangel Jeremiel's** name means "mercy of God." Jeremiel is an inspirer who motivates us to devote ourselves to spiritual acts of service. He's also involved with the process of attaining Divine wisdom. Call upon Jeremiel if you feel "stuck" spiritually, and to regain enthusiasm about your spiritual path and Divine mission.

— **Archangel Jophiel's** name means "beauty of God." Also known as Iophiel and Zophiel, he is the Patron Archangel of Artists, who helps us see and maintain beauty in life. Call upon Jophiel before beginning any artistic project. Since Jophiel is involved in beautifying the planet by cleansing it of pollution, ask him for assignments to help in this vital mission.

— **Archangel Metatron's** name means "Angel of the Presence." He is thought to be the youngest and the tallest of the archangels, and the only archangel who once walked upon the earth as a man (as the prophet Enoch). Metatron works with Mother Mary to help children, both living and crossed over. Call upon Metatron for any kind of assistance you may need with your children. His intervention often involves helping youngsters open their spiritual awareness and understanding.

— **Archangel Michael's** name means "he who is as God" or "he who looks like God." He is the archangel who releases the effects of fear from the planet and its inhabitants. Michael is the Patron Archangel of Police Officers, and he gives all of us the courage and backbone to follow our truth and fulfill our Divine mission. Call upon Michael if you feel afraid or confused about your personal safety, your Divine mission, or making a necessary life change. You can also call upon Michael to help you fix any mechanical or electrical problems.

— **Archangel Raguel's** name means "friend of God." He is often called the Archangel of Justice and Fairness, and he is the champion of underdogs. Call upon Raguel whenever you feel that you're being overpowered or manipulated. Raguel will intervene by giving you guidance about how to attain balanced power and fairness within the structure of your personal and community relationships. Also call upon Raguel on behalf of another person who is being unfairly treated.

— **Archangel Raphael's** name means "God heals," because Raphael is in charge of physical healings. He helps all healers, including would-be ones. Call upon Raphael for any injuries or illnesses related to yourself or another (including animals). Also call on Raphael to help with your healing work, including education and building a private practice. In addition, Archangel Raphael helps those who are traveling, so call upon him to ensure a harmonious and safe journey.

— **Archangel Raziel's** name means "secret of God." Raziel is said to stand very near to God, so he hears all Divine conversations about universal secrets and mysteries. Raziel wrote these secrets into a document that he gave to Adam, which eventually ended up in the hands of the prophets Enoch and Samuel. Call upon Raziel whenever you wish to understand esoteric material, or to engage in alchemy or manifestation.

— **Archangel Sandalphon's** name means "brother," because he is the twin brother of Archangel Metatron. Sandolphon is the Archangel of Music and Prayer. He assists Archangel Michael to clear away fear and the effects of fear (probably with music). Put on some soothing music, and call upon Sandolphon to dispel any spiritual confusion.

— **Archanel Uriel's** name means "God is light." As he explains in his message earlier in the book (see page 75), Archangel Uriel pours light upon a troubling situation, which illuminates our problem-solving abilities. Call upon Uriel whenever you get into a sticky situation and you need to think clearly and find answers.

— **Archangel Zadkiel's** name means "righteousness of God." Zadkiel helps us attain freedom through forgiveness, and he is known as the Patron Archangel of Those Who Forgive. For this reason, call upon Zadkiel to help you release toxins from anger and unforgiveness (toward yourself or another). Zadkiel helps us to view others with compassion, instead of judgment.

Ascended Masters

Ascended masters are beings who walked upon the earth as great leaders, teachers, and healers, and who continue to help us from their vantage point in the spirit world. They include the famous, such as Jesus, Moses, Buddha, Quan Yin, Mary, Yogananda, Ashtar, and the saints; and the not-so-famous—such as yogis who transcended physical restrictions during their lifetime, pioneering inventors, and unsung heroes. With bigger-than-life love in their hearts and a steadfast devotion to us, the ascended masters help anyone who calls upon them.

The Nature Angels

Often referred to as fairies, elementals, or devas, the nature angels are as much God's angels as are the guardian and archangels. Viewed with suspicion, though, they're often disregarded and misunderstood. I recently visited a large bookstore and happily noted all of the angel books on a shelf that was specially marked "Angels." But I wondered, *Where are the books about fairies?* I looked all around the New Age and Spirituality areas without finding one fairy book. I finally found them in a large section called "Mythology." I felt the sting of outrage on behalf of the fairies, and I understood why I'd been given the assignment to help bring their word forward in my books and workshops.

Fairies are believed to be mischievous at best, and evil at worst. Unlike guardian angels or archangels, the nature angels do have egos. They are denser angels who live closer to Earth, and those beings who live on Earth usually do have an ego after all.

The nature angels, including the fairies, are God's environmental angels. They oversee the earth's atmosphere, landscape, bodies of water, and animals. If you're someone who respects the environment by, for instance, recycling and picking up litter, the fairies will accord you great respect. If, on top of that, you go the extra measure, such as being kind to animals and using nontoxic cleaning compounds, the fairies will be thrilled to meet and work with you. The nature angels scan each person with whom they come into contact, and they know instantly about your level of commitment to the environment. As soon as you begin communicating with the nature angels, they will attempt to enlist you as an aide in their environmental campaign.

Those whose life purpose involves helping animals or the environment often have fairies or other elementals near them, acting as guardian angels. These elementals are with the humans, in addition to their guardian angels and spirit guides. I've found that these guardian elemental spirits behave themselves quite well and don't interfere with their humans' free will or happiness. Their interventions are usually limited to proddings to get involved in environmental causes and to engage in free-spirited body movement.

About Our Deceased Loved Ones and Spirit Guides

If you've lost loved ones, chances are that those people have spent time with you after they've crossed over. They may even be with you on a regular basis. After all, in addition to angels, archangels, and ascended masters, we also have deceased loved ones with us to help and assist. They include relatives who passed before your birth, deceased loved ones with whom you shared a close bond, or those from your past who teach you a special skill for your life's purpose. A departed being who stays with you continuously is called your "spirit guide." Usually, we have one or two spirit guides.

When a person passes away, they're eventually given the option of performing service work, both to expand their own spiritual progress and to help others. Some people volunteer to become spirit guides to their living loved ones. They usually elect to stay until the end of their living person's physical life. Time measurement is different in Heaven, so if you live to be 90, it feels like a much shorter time period to your spirit guides.

Spirit guides are with you because they love and care about you. In addition, you may have a similar life purpose to the deceased loved one who is by your side. Being with you is a way to vicariously fulfill your spirit guide's life purpose if they didn't fulfill it while living. If you were named after your dear departed Aunt Annette, chances are that she is your spirit guide. Namesakes nearly always stay with us. Perhaps we were named after that person because our parents intuitively realized our soul-path similarities.

So, when Aunt Annette decides to be your spirit guide, she first must go through the equivalent of a spiritual counselor training program. In that Heavenly school, Aunt Annette learns how to be with you in a supportive way, without interfering with your free will. She learns how to travel the astral plane and still be within earshot should you ever call for her help. Aunt Annette learns how to communicate with you through your strongest spiritual communication channel, such as your dreams, your inner voice, your gut feelings, or your intellectual insights. It takes time to train to become a spirit guide. That's why recently deceased loved ones aren't with us continuously. Only someone who has gone through extensive training can be with us night and day.

Let's say that Aunt Annette was a very successful newspaper reporter and you're an aspiring writer. In fact, writing is part of your life's purpose. So when you ask Heaven, "What's my mission in life?," Aunt Annette telepathically encourages you to write. Of course, your auntie is only doing this because she knows what God's Divine mission is for you.

Sometimes people will ask me if it's okay to talk with the dead. They may quote from the Torah, which warns of speaking to the dead and mediums. I can understand these warnings, because it's a mistake to turn our lives over to deceased loved ones, just like it's a mistake to turn our lives over to *living* loved ones.

Our higher self, in conjunction with our Creator, is whom we want to turn our life over to. Our deceased loved ones can definitely help us, but they're not automatically saints, angels, or psychics just because their souls have crossed over. However, they can work in conjunction with God, the Holy Spirit, the ascended masters, and the angels to help us fulfill God's will (which is one with our higher self's will). I think the main reason to contact deceased loved ones is for that extra boost of help they can provide, as well as to maintain, heal, or deepen the relationship.

For Those Who Are Adopted

I'm often asked about the spirit guides of adoptees. I've found that people who were adopted have more angels and spirit guides with them than non-adoptees. An adopted person always has a spirit guide who is a deceased relative from their birth family—I've never seen an exception to this. It could be the deceased parent, or a sibling, grandparent, aunt, or uncle. It doesn't matter whether the adopted person ever met this birth relative or not. The family bond is there, regardless of whether a personal relationship was forged while living.

In addition, the adopted person has deceased loved ones from the friends and adopted family members whom they've been with along the way. I believe that adopted people have more angels than normal to protect them, and help them adjust to the life changes that result from the process of adoption.

Deepening Your Relationship with Deceased Loved Ones

"Are my departed loved ones okay?" is a question I hear continually. The reason people ask is simple: the fear that a deceased loved one is in some sort of "hellish" place, literally or figuratively. Yet, my readings find that 90 percent of deceased people are doing just fine, thank you. Their only discomfort has to do with you and me, especially if we're grief-stricken to the point of obsession or emotional paralysis. Your deceased loved ones are going on with their lives, and they want you to do the same. If you hold back your spiritual progress or happiness due to grief, your deceased loved one is held back in similar ways.

In fact, it's safe to say that the only problem most people in Heaven have is . . . *us!* If we would go on to live happy, productive lives, our deceased loved ones would sing and party in Heaven in joyful celebration.

In Heaven, souls feel wonderful physically. All illness, injury, and disability disappear once the body is gone. The soul is intact and in perfect health. The soul still feels like him- or herself, but without the heaviness and pain of having a body.

In Heaven, souls feel wonderful emotionally, too. Gone are all of the financial and time constraints, and there are no more pressures or concerns (unless we are inordinately desolate and pull our departed loved ones down emotionally). A soul in Heaven is free to manifest any situation or condition, such as world travel, a beautiful home, volunteer work, and time with family and friends (living and deceased).

"But what if my departed loved ones are mad at me?" I'm frequently asked. People worry that crossed-over friends and family members are angry with them because they:

- weren't there for the dying person toward the end of their life, or for their last dying breath;

- were involved in decisions to stop artificial life-support systems;

- are involved in lifestyle choices that they believe their deceased loved ones wouldn't approve of;

- fought with family members over inheritance issues;

- could have prevented the death, or that they were somehow to blame;

- haven't yet found, or brought to justice, the person who is seemingly responsible for a murder or accident; and/or

- had an argument with the person shortly before their death.

The fact is, though, that during all of my thousands of readings, I've never met a deceased person who was angry about any of the above matters. In Heaven, you release a lot of the concerns that weigh you down on Earth. In Heaven, you have better clarity about people's true motivations, so your deceased loved ones have a deeper understanding of why you acted (or still do act) in certain ways. Instead of judging you, they view you with compassion. They only interfere with your behaviors (such as addictions) if they see that your lifestyle is killing you or preventing you from fulfilling your life's purpose.

And don't worry that Grandpa is watching when you shower or make love. Crossed-over souls aren't voyeurs. In fact, there's some evidence that spirit guides don't see our physical selves on Earth; they see our energy and light bodies instead. So, a spirit guide simply sees your true thoughts and feelings during each circumstance.

Since spirit guides are truly aware of how you actually feel and think, there's no need to hide your worries from your departed loved ones. Let's say that you have conflicted feelings over your father's death. You're angry because Dad's incessant cigarette smoking and alcohol drinking contributed to his too-early demise. But you feel guilty, because you believe it's "wrong" to be angry at a dead person, especially your dad.

Your father knows just how you feel, because he's able to read your mind and heart from his vantage point in Heaven. Our deceased loved ones ask us to come clean with them—to have a heart-to-heart discussion about our unfinished anger, fears, guilt, and worries. You can have this discussion by writing a letter to your departed one, by thinking the thoughts you want to convey, or by speaking aloud.

You can communicate with your deceased loved ones anytime and anywhere. Their souls aren't located at the cemetery. The soul is free and travels to whoever calls it. And don't worry that you're disturbing your loved one's peace. Everyone wants to heal unfinished business in relationships whether they're living or deceased, so your departed one is just as happy and motivated about this discussion as you are. (You can find more information about communicating with Heaven in the last chapter of this book.)

Animal Angels

Would it surprise you to discover that among the deceased loved ones who watch over you are some of your beloved pets? Your dogs, cats, horses, and any other animals you deeply loved stay with you after their physical passing. The love bond that you shared with your pets when they were living acts like a leash that keeps them eternally by your side, long after death.

When I give workshops, I tell audience members about the dogs and cats I see running and playing throughout the room. Usually we can figure out pretty quickly which dog belongs to which person, because the dogs stay by their owner's side. These reunions, in which audience members discover that Rover is still around, are quite touching and emotional. They discover that their dogs have the same personalities, appearance, and behaviors that they did while living. If the dog was playful, hyperactive, friendly, well groomed, or amazingly calm while alive, she maintains these characteristics after physical death. Playful dogs jump in piles of etheric leaves and chase after balls. Whether these leaves, balls, and other playthings are conjured by the dogs' imagination, I don't know.

Cats stay with their owners, too, although they usually don't stick as closely to a human's side as a dog does due to their independence. So, at my workshops, it's difficult for me to tell which cats belong to which owners. I have to rely on describing the various cats running around the room, and having their owners "claim" them.

Many of my audience members report that they've seen or felt apparitions of their deceased pets. For instance, you might feel Fluffy the cat jump on your bed, or sense Red the dog lying on the couch beside you. You might even see them dart across the room, out of the corner of your eye. This is because the corner of our eye is more sensitive to light and movement than the front of our eye, so we often see psychic visions out of this area. When we turn to view the image from the front, though, it seems to disappear.

I've seen a few horses and even one guinea pig hanging around people like guardian angels. These were beloved pets to their owners, and the animals continue to stand loyally next to their "people." The animals help by infusing us with their Divine energy of love, and also providing companionship that maybe only our unconscious is aware of.

I've also seen spirit totem animals with people who have past-life connections to Native American cultures. These are eagles, wolves, and bears who circle their human's head, giving them protection and natural wisdom. I've seen dolphins with people who are involved in ecological concerns, as well as unicorns around people who are highly attuned to nature and the elemental kingdom. I've never seen a pet goldfish hanging around someone, but then again, goldfish go through a very different sort of tube of light at the end of their lives, don't they?!

You can maintain communication with all of your deceased loved ones, including your pets, through the processes described in the last chapter of this book.

◦∾ Messages from Children in Heaven ∿◦

There's probably nothing more tragic than saying "good-bye" to your child, yet children's souls are very lively in Heaven, and they definitely live on in very happy and meaningful ways. For the last several years, I've limited my private angel-therapy practice to readings for parents of children who have died. I've learned a great deal talking to children on the Other Side.

Losing a child brings up more parental guilt than just about anything I've ever witnessed. Most parents become basket cases, wondering whether they could have prevented—or whether they in some way caused—their child's death. The parents hound themselves with "if only's": "If only I hadn't let Amy drive the car that night," "If only I'd paid more attention to Dan when he said that he was unhappy," or "If only I'd been stricter about letting Jacob stay out so late at night."

Of course, berating yourself won't bring your child's body back to life. However, I'd like to share some information with you that may help your heart to heal.

— *Young children have a different perspective on death.* Children who are five years old or younger don't have a concept of death the way that we do. That's why it's so difficult to explain the permanence of a loved one's passing to a toddler. "But *when* is Grandpa coming back?" the toddler will continually ask, no matter how many times you explain that he's now in Heaven.

So, when infants and children pass over, they don't realize that they're dead. After all, they feel happy and alive. *Why is everyone crying?* they wonder. Since they don't know that they're dead, these children rush to the aid of their bereaved family members, offering etheric gifts to cheer them up. One time when I was giving a reading to a mother who had lost her four-year-old daughter, the mother began sobbing inconsolably. From the spirit world, the little girl began drawing paintings of rainbows to comfort her mom. As she handed each rainbow painting to her mother, I reported the occurrence.

"She loved painting rainbows when she was living," the mother said to me wistfully. "She knew that they always brought a smile to my face, too."

— *Children don't hold grudges in Heaven.* I've never met a deceased child (or adult, for that matter) who blames you for their death. Even murder victims are very forgiving of their murderers, realizing that holding on to anger only hurts *them.* The murder victim may help to incarcerate a murderer, though—not out of revenge, but to prevent additional murders from occurring.

Children who are aborted don't blame their parents, and they don't realize that they're dead either. In fact, the souls of children who don't grow to full-term births because of abortion, miscarriage, or stillbirth stay by their mother's side. Those souls then have "first dibs" on the next body that the mother conceives. So, if you've lost an infant or fetus and have since had another child, chances are good that this is the same soul. If the mother doesn't conceive additional children, that soul then grows up next to the mother and acts as a spirit guide. Or, the child's soul may enter the physical world and come into its mother's family in another way, such as adoption, or by becoming the woman's niece or nephew.

— *A child's soul can hold great wisdom.* Even though children's bodies are small, it doesn't mean that their souls are young, hapless, or naive. So we need to consider that the child's soul may have had some responsibility in the timing of the death. The text of the spiritual tome *A Course in Miracles* says, "No one dies without his own consent," and I have found that to be true. Ask any nurse or doctor, and they'll tell you stories of people who died from minor illnesses because they willed themselves to. They'll also tell you uplifting stories about people who decided to live, despite all medical odds being against them.

As difficult as it may be to accept, your child may have made the decision to go home to Heaven before you were ready for him or her to leave. In my book *Angel Therapy*, the angels said that they don't understand where we got the idea that everyone is supposed to live to be 90 years old!

As I mentioned earlier, before our conception, we decide along with our angels and guides what ages we will be when we pass from our physical bodies. One teenage boy told me that following his car accident, he was given a life-or-death choice by his angels, who showed him the consequences of each choice. During my reading with this boy and his living mother, he said to them through me:

> *"I gave you a gift by choosing to die, even though you may not understand it. I was shown that, if I had chosen to live, I would have been severely disabled. I was shown how stressful that would have been to you, your finances, and to me. I was shown that the stress would affect your marriage. I would have felt helpless and guilty had I*

chosen to live! So please forgive me, but I made the choice to leave my body. The angels showed me that, as painful as it would be for you, you would eventually recover and go on. They showed me that you and Dad would stay married and supportive of each other.

"So please accept my gift. Please accept my choice and decision! You were always proud of me in the past, and I need you to be proud of me now for this decision that I've made. Please believe me that I'm very, very happy here."

The mother told me that, when her son was in the operating room following his car accident, the doctor reported that his vital signs were sporadic. "He said it was like having a tug-of-war with my son's life, where my son would come back into his body for a while, only to leave a moment later and then come back." The mother vowed to accept her son's decision with as much grace as she could muster. I counseled her to work with prayer and a grief-support group to buoy up her faith that her son's death was not in vain, and to know that he was happy and at peace in Heaven.

— *All suffering is now over.* Many parents drive themselves crazy imagining that their child suffered terribly prior to their death. I won't sugarcoat it—many people do suffer physical pain and sheer terror during the death process. Fortunately, God's mercy has created some safeguards that help us shut down awareness of overwhelming pain. The human body will faint, the person will disassociate (go somewhere else in consciousness), or the spirit will be removed from the body before the pain gets too horrible. I find that most parents' imaginings are ten times worse than the actual suffering the child undergoes.

— *Children are never alone in Heaven.* Grandparents, aunts, uncles, beloved pets, and other children surround any child who has passed away. Usually, children live in Heaven with relatives whom they knew upon Earth, and/or those who were the child's spirit guides. In Heaven, you can manifest any type of home that you like, so the children in Heaven have relatively normal lives, are in comfortable homes, and are surrounded by loving family members and friends. I have never met a child in Heaven who was alone.

— *The vast majority of young people who commit suicide adjust very well in Heaven.* The myth is that people who commit suicide go to hell and suffer for their "sin." The movie *What Dreams May Come* with Robin Williams seemed to underscore this myth (although I believe the scriptwriter was making a metaphor about suicide, many people I talk to take the portrayal literally).

Suicide *is* frowned upon in Heaven, because it's wasting a body that could be used in service of the Light. However, no one judges suicide victims, and they certainly aren't cast into any hell or dungeon. They can create their own hell-like situation through the extreme guilt they feel once they realize how much pain they caused their surviving family members. Yet, the majority of deceased people I've talked to following their suicides rapidly forgive themselves and whomever they were angry with.

Angels and guides surround these individuals like mental-health counselors. Your prayers also help the person's spiritual upliftment and healing. Very often, the person is assigned some form of community-service work to balance the karma of the pain that the suicide engendered.

Parental guilt seems to go hand in hand with rearing children, and this guilt is certainly compounded when our children become ill, get injured, or pass away. However, *A Course in Miracles* reminds us that guilt isn't a form of love; it is actually an attack in disguise. When we feel guilt, we're attacking ourselves and debasing the other person's free will. Guilt is often arrogance at its worst, when we fantasize that we could have swooped in and saved the day. Perhaps we could have, perhaps not. But what purpose does it serve to second-guess it after the fact? Our deceased loved ones, especially our children, want us to be happy. And the best route to happiness that I know of is through giving service using our natural talents, passions, or interests.

This service work can be a living memorial to a deceased child, something to make meaning out of the seemingly senseless death. For instance, you could plant a tree in the child's honor, organize a 5K marathon to raise funds for other children in similar situations, give a speech to parents' groups on a topic relevant to your child's life and death, put an organ-donor card on the back of your driver's license (making sure that you also inform your family about your desire to become a donor), write an article about your child, name a star after him or her, or start a fund in your child's name. Whether the effort is seemingly small or monumentally heroic on your part, your child will appreciate it very much. He or she will likely help you with the project as well.

Life Goes On

In the next few chapters, you'll read about some methods to keep your relationship with your loved ones alive through spiritual communication. As we've seen in the last two chapters, our deceased loved ones want us to continue our lives in healthy, happy, and meaningful ways. And that, perhaps, is the best living monument we could make to them.

How to Know If It's Truly Your Angels or Just Your Imagination

A little girl stares at the space near her left shoulder, having a seemingly one-sided conversation.

"Who are you talking to, sweetheart?" her mother asks.

"My angel," the girl replies matter-of-factly.

The girl's mother recounted to me later, "The funny thing is, we aren't a religious family, and we've never discussed angels in front of her. As far as I know, she hasn't had any exposure to angels."

I've heard similar stories from parents all around the world. Children are definitely more receptive to seeing and hearing their angels than the average adult. And why is that? In my research, I've found that the primary reason is that *children don't care whether the angel and its message constitute reality or fantasy.* They simply enjoy the experience without questioning its validity. Perhaps that's why a study by Dr. William MacDonald of the University of Ohio found that children had more verifiable psychic experiences than any other age group.

We adults get so uptight about whether we're imagining an angel's presence that we often dismiss legitimate Divine guidance! If we could be as a child and suspend disbelief for a while, we could enjoy deeper and richer experiences of God and the angelic kingdom.

However, our adult left brain often rules the roost and demands proof and evidence. And perhaps painful experiences have made us guarded in this respect. We want guarantees that our lives really will improve before we're willing to quit our jobs and become self-employed, or leave our spouse and search for our true soulmate.

Fortunately, some distinguishing characteristics help us to tell true angelic experiences from wishful thinking (or Earthbound spirits). Angelic experiences occur to us through our four Divine senses: vision, hearing, thoughts, and feelings. We all receive angelic messages through these senses. However, we have one primary sense that we're particularly attuned to. For instance, I am a highly visual person, so most of my angelic experiences come as visions. Other people might be more attuned to their gut feelings, their thoughts, or their inner ears.

Feeling Heaven's Messages

An emotional or physical "feeling" is the way that most people experience their angels. When you're unsure whether you're really experiencing an angelic visit or message, check for these signs:

A True Angelic Experience Involving Feelings	Imagination or False Guidance Involving Feelings
Feels warm and cuddly, like a loving hug	Feels cold and prickly
Makes you feel safe, even if it's warning you of danger	Makes you feel afraid and panicky
Often accompanied by disembodied fragrances of flowers, or of your deceased loved one's distinct scent	No sense of smell associated with the experience, or an unfamiliar and unpleasant smell

A True Angelic Experience Involving Feelings (cont'd.)	Imagination or False Guidance Involving Feelings (cont'd.)
May feel an indent in the couch or bed, as if someone has just sat next to you	May feel like a being is sexually fondling you
May feel air-pressure or temperature changes	Room may feel ice-cold
Feels like someone touches your head, hair, or shoulder	Sense of being all alone
May feel sleepy or hyper afterward	Normal feeling returns quickly
A gut feeling that "this is real"	A gut feeling that the experience wasn't real
Repetitious and consistent gut feelings to make a certain life change, or to take a certain step	Gut feelings to change your life, but with changing themes and ideas that come from desperation, not from Divine guidance
A feeling that a familiar person is next to you, such as sensing a particular deceased loved one	No sense of familiarity to the feeling
Feels natural, as if the experience is coming to you freely	Feels forced, as if you're willing the experience or guidance to happen

Receiving Heaven's Messages As Thoughts

Your experiences with your angels may involve ideas, revelations, or thoughts rather than your feelings. Many of the world's great thinkers and inventors get their innovative ideas from the ethers. Here's how to sort the true from the false:

A True Angelic Experience Involving Thoughts	Imagination or False Guidance Involving Thoughts
Consistent and repetitive	Random and ever-changing
Central theme of how you can help solve a problem or help others	Central theme of how you would get rich or famous
Positive and empowering	Discouraging and abusive
Gives you explicit instructions about what step to take right now, and will give you instructions for subsequent steps once you complete the first ones	Has you thinking about worst-case scenarios
Exciting ideas that energize you	Depressing or frightening thoughts
Idea comes out-of-the-blue, in response to prayer	Idea comes slowly, in response to worry
Idea involves you taking human steps and doing some work	Idea is a get-rich-quick scheme
Idea rings true and makes sense	Idea seems hollow and ill-conceived

A True Angelic Experience Involving Thoughts (cont'd.)	Imagination or False Guidance Involving Thoughts (cont'd.)
Idea is consistent with your natural interests, passions, or talents	Idea is unrelated to anything you've previously done or been interested in
Knowing that a certain deceased loved one is near, without seeing them	The idea is primarily motivated by a desire to escape a current situation, rather than how to help others

Hearing Heaven's Messages

It's a trite Psychology 101 joke that hearing voices is a sign of insanity. In contrast, many of the world's saints, sages, and great inventors have received guidance in the form of a disembodied voice. Prior to my carjacking, I heard a loud, clear voice warn me. And thousands of people have told me of receiving similar warnings that saved them or their loved ones from danger, in a way that defies normal explanation.

The difference between hearing a true Divine voice, hearing the imagination, or having a hallucination is clear and distinct. I'll give you quite a bit of information about the differences between messages from your angels and your imagination. As to the distinction of hallucinations, several scientists point out key distinctions between the two:

- Researcher D. J. West gave this definition of the difference between a hallucination and a true psychic experience: "Pathological hallucinations tend to keep to certain rather rigid patterns, to occur repeatedly during a manifest illness but not at other times, and to be accompanied by other symptoms and particularly by disturbances of consciousness and loss of awareness of the normal surroundings. The spontaneous psychic [now often called "paranormal"] experience is more often an isolated event disconnected from any illness or known disturbance and definitely not accompanied by any loss of contact with normal surroundings."[1]

- Researcher Bruce Greyson, M.D., studied 68 people who were prescreened clinically to rule out schizophrenia. Dr. Greyson found that exactly half of these subjects reported having an apparition experience, where they had seen a deceased loved one with their physical eyes open.[2]

- Psychic researchers Karlis Osis, Ph.D., and Erlendur Haraldsson, Ph.D., noted that during most hallucinations, the person believes that they're seeing a living human being. During psychic experiences involving visions, the person believes that they're seeing a celestial being, such as an angel, a deceased loved one, or an ascended master.[3]

Heaven may speak to us through a loud, disembodied voice outside our head; a quiet inner voice inside our head; a conversation that we "happen" to overhear; or by hearing music in our minds or over and over again on the radio.

A True Angelic Experience Involving Hearing	Imagination or False Guidance Involving Hearing
Sentences usually begin with the word *You* or *We*	Sentences usually begin with the word *I*
There's a sense that someone else is talking to you, even if it sounds like your own voice	It feels like you're talking to yourself
The message is readily apparent in how it's related to your immediate concerns or questions	The message is muddy, cryptic, or unclear
The voice is to-the-point and blunt	The voice is wordy and vague
The voice is loving and positive, even if it's warning you of danger	The voice is taunting, alarming, or cruel
The voice asks you to take immediate action, including changing your thoughts or attitude to be more loving	The voice gossips and speculates about others
Hearing a voice call your name upon awakening	Hearing abusive words
Hearing strains of disembodied, beautiful "celestial" music	Hearing loud, unpleasant noises or discordant music
Hearing a message about self-improvement, or helping others	Hearing a message to hurt yourself or others

Seeing Heaven's Messages

Your angelic experiences may also involve what you see, either while awake, asleep, or meditating. Here's how to sort the true visions from the false ones:

A True Angelic Experience Involving Seeing	Imagination or False Guidance Involving Seeing
Dream visitations seem more than real, with vivid colors and emotions	Dreams seem ordinary and forgettable
Seeing sparkles or flashes of light, or colored mists	Seeing worst-case-scenario visions, without being given instructions on how to avoid the situation
A feeling of spontaneity and naturalness to the vision	A feeling that you're forcing the vision to occur
Repetitive instances of seeing a feather, coin, bird, butterfly, rainbow, number sequence, and so on, beyond chance occurrences	Looking for a sign, but finding inconsistency, or forcing the meaning that you want onto what you see
Seeing a service-oriented vision of yourself helping others	Seeing an ego-centered vision of yourself gaining at the expense of others

Paying Attention to the Messages

Whether your angelic messages come to you as a vision, a voice, an idea, a feeling, or a combination of these four elements, you can distinguish true from false guidance by paying attention to the characteristics in this chapter's charts. Be assured that if you're facing danger before it's your time to go, your angels will give you very loud and clear guidance, regardless of the form in which it appears. Guidance about daily life might appear more subtly, but in the following chapters, you'll read about ways to amplify its intensity and clarity.

Everyone has an equal ability to communicate with their angels, because everyone is equally "gifted" spiritually. Some people may appear to be more psychically gifted than others; however, that's only because that person has been willing to listen, believe, and trust the input of their spiritual senses.

The single biggest block I find in my psychic-development students is that they try too hard to make an angel experience happen. They want to see and hear an angel so desperately that they strain to see and hear. Anytime we strain, though, we're coming from a place of fear. It could be the fear that "maybe I won't be able to see or hear," or that "maybe I don't have angels," or some other vague ego-based fear. The ego isn't psychic at all, being entirely fear based. Only the love-based higher self within each of us is able to communicate with the Divine.

So, the more you can relax, the more easily you'll be able to consciously commune with your angels. Breath is a wonderful starting place, as is optimism akin to what many children whom I meet say about angel encounters: "*Of course* I have angels. Everyone does!" Children don't care whether they're imagining their angel visions; they simply enjoy and accept them. As a result, children easily see and hear their guardian angels. If we would stop worrying whether our Divine connection is real or not, we would overcome the ego's blocks and enjoy our higher self's natural gifts.

The angels say, *"Fear is a natural predator of the psychic domain. Fear controls and robs your psyche of its creative control and asks if you would allow it to dominate your moods, your schedule, and your decisions. It weakens you who are all-powerful. Your decision-making capability is impaired at its behest. Allow no fear to 'inter-fear' with your domain of happiness, for that is God's kingdom of great blessings. You're more powerful than any fearful force. Your Divine willingness can out-will any darkness that the world has ever seen. Your Creator's light will always blind away any darkness if you will but focus on this light within your mind."*

So, instead of doubting our ability to connect with our angels, let's look at how we already do receive messages from Heaven, and how we can enhance that connection even more. In the next few chapters, we'll look at how to increase the volume and clarity of your angels' messages.

---

[1]West, D.J. (1960). "Visionary and Hallucinatory Experiences: A Comparative Appraisal." *International Journal of Parapsychology*, Vol. 2, No. 1, pp. 89–100.

[2]Stevenson, I. (1983). "Do We Need a New Word to Supplement 'Hallucination'?" *American Journal of Psychiatry*, Vol. 140, No. 12, pp. 1609–11.

[3]Osis, K. and Harraldsson, E. (1997). *At the Hour of Death*. Third Edition (Norwalk, CT: Hastings House).

How to Feel Your Angels

When angels or deceased loved ones come extra-close, you can feel their presence. Many people I interview can recall when they felt a specific deceased loved one nearby. Most say something like, "Yes, I could feel my mother with me the other night. It felt so real, but I still wonder if I was just imagining it or not."

We tend to discount our feelings and not trust them. How many times have you had a gut feeling to *not* get involved in a certain relationship, or to *not* take a certain job, or to *not* buy a certain item, or to *not* drive a certain route? But then you overrode your feelings, did it anyway, and later regretted it.

Of course, whether or not we listen to our feelings, such situations give us opportunities to learn to trust and follow our gut feelings the next time.

It's the same process when it comes to communing with your angels and deceased loved ones. It has to do with trusting that your feelings are a legitimate and accurate divining device, which God installed in you. In the case of discerning a deceased loved one's presence, it involves trusting that you really can distinguish one person's presence from another. In that way, we're all naturally gifted psychic mediums.

The way that we do mediumship for strangers is the same feeling-based way that you can conduct mediumship for yourself. When I conduct mediumship for a total stranger, I first hold the intention of contacting that person's deceased loved ones. Then, that person's primary deceased loved one will show up. Most of my contact with the being is visual, because that's my basic channel of Divine communication. But a lot of my communication is also feeling based.

After physical death, a person still retains the energy pattern and physical dimensions of their former self, and that's what a medium sees. People who see apparitions of their deceased loved ones say that the people look just like they did when they were living, only younger and more radiant. I've found that the energy patterns of deceased people are similar to wavelengths of the color spectrum. Older people have slower and longer energy wavelengths, while youngsters have faster-vibrating energy waves. And females have faster energy wavelengths than males. So, it *is* possible to conduct mediumship solely by feeling, based on perceiving these sonarlike waves.

Here's how to do that: Each person has a unique "fingerprint" to their personality, persona, behaviors, habits, and other distinguishing characteristics. Have you ever walked into your home, and—even though you live with several people and have no physical evidence—you can feel who else is in the house as you go in? Or, let's say that you're in the kitchen fixing a meal and you hear the front door open. Without using logic, you can feel who entered the home. Another example is when you go into a room full of people and you can sense the mood of the crowd.

In the same way, when your deceased loved ones are near you, they have a unique energy fingerprint that you can feel. When I conduct mediumship sessions, I find that 90 percent of my clients already know which deceased loved ones are nearby. My clients come to me to merely validate their feelings. For some reason, they aren't willing to accept the validity of their own feelings until an outside "expert" confirms them.

You can imagine how difficult it must be for professional psychics such as myself to stick out our necks and publicly conduct mediumship sessions on television, at workshops, and on radio programs. Most of the time, when I'm doing a public mediumship session, I have no idea about the meaning of the information that I'm relaying to my client. Yet, I trust my gut feelings enough to speak aloud about the information I'm given, and 99 percent of the time, my client will say, "Yes, that's exactly right!" It has taken me a lot of practice, prayer, a brush with death, and many trials and errors to reach this state of confidence in my gut feelings. My prayer is that we'll all reach that state of trust in our emotional and physical feelings.

Common Ways That We Feel a Spiritual Presence

Here are some of the common ways that we connect with our angels and deceased loved ones through our feelings:

- Smelling a deceased loved one's favorite cologne, or other distinctive scent

- Smelling flowers or smoke, when there are no blossoms or fire nearby

- Feeling that someone has touched you, stroked your hair, pushed you, protected you, tucked you in, or is hugging you

- Feeling someone sit next to you, and feeling an indent on the sofa or bed where that deceased person or animal has just sat or jumped up

- Feeling an air-pressure change, a sense of tightness around the head, a feeling that something is pounding on your forehead, a sense of some spiritual essence moving through your head, or a feeling similar to being pulled underwater

- Air temperature changes

- A sudden feeling of euphoria or bliss

- A gut feeling that this experience is surreal

- A feeling of familiarity comes over you, as a deceased person you have long known hovers nearby

True angelic experiences feel warm, safe, loving, and comfortable, while false experiences make you feel cold, prickly, and afraid. False experiences can originate from either the ego or from an Earthbound spirit. Earthbound spirits are beings who are afraid to go to the Divine Light in the afterlife plane, either because they're attached to Earthly life (possessions or addictions, for example) or because they're afraid of being judged by God and cast into "hell." So, the being stays near to Earth and can interfere with a living person's happiness. More information on Earthbound spirits can be found in my book *The Lightworker's Way* (Hay House, 1997).

A "touchy" subject (no pun intended) is that some Earthbound spirits will approach living persons for sexual favors. I've met many widows and widowers who are comforted by having continued sexual relationships with their deceased husband or wife. Yet, this is entirely different from the slew of New Age women I've recently encountered who report freely having sexual relationships with nonphysical strangers in the spirit world. I consider these encounters to be spiritually oppressive to the living, as a high-level spirit or angel would never approach a human being for sexual favors. While the living women whom I've interviewed nearly always report a positive sexual experience in these instances, the message that I've strongly received is that these activities encourage low-level Earthbound entities to stay with us. They can also create barriers in meeting a new boyfriend or girlfriend, as new suitors unconsciously sense the presence of another lover who is already on the scene. No one can be spiritually "raped" without their own consent, fortunately. But if you are hit upon by a being (living or deceased) and you need help, please call upon Archangel Michael to escort this being away. He will help you immediately.

Low-level, imaginary encounters leave us feeling empty, while true encounters remind us that our angels and deceased loved ones are near us always. How do you tell if it's an angel or a deceased loved one who's helping you? An angel's energy will pull you upward in a nondescript way. You'll suddenly feel a rush of love or joy without knowing why. Or you'll get a strong gut feeling, and if you follow it, your life will change in miraculous ways. A deceased loved one will have a distinctly familiar feeling, and you'll likely be able to identify the person, perhaps with an accompanying feeling of a hug, a touch, an air-pressure change, or a distinct aroma.

You can also use your feelings to "test drive" an intuitive sensation and notice how you react. For instance, let's say that a gut feeling is urging you to move to a new area. You're conflicted, however, wondering how such a move would affect your family, friends, and career. Even though some of these factors aren't clear to you, you can "try on your future" and get a better grip on your Divine guidance.

As you imagine what it would be like to stay living where you are, focus on your feelings. Does your heart feel full of relief, sadness, joy, or some other emotion? Does any part of your body tighten or relax in response to the mental image?

Now, compare your emotional and physical feelings when you imagine what it would be like to move. Your feelings are very accurate gauges of your soul's desires and your Divine will, which is one with God's will.

How to Increase Your Clairsentience

If you're not normally feeling oriented, you can use the following methods to open this important channel of Divine communication. When we become more sensitive to our emotions and physical sensations, life becomes richer, relationships deepen, we feel greater compassion and Divine love, we understand others more readily, we become more balanced, and we're more apt to notice and follow our intuition.

Here are some steps that can increase your clairsentience:

— *Sleep next to clear quartz crystals.* You can purchase a clear quartz crystal "point" (a cylinder with a point at the end) fairly inexpensively at any metaphysical bookstore or gem show. Place the crystal in sunlight for at least four hours to clear away any psychic residue from its previous owner. Then, put one or more of these crystal points on your nightstand or beneath your bed. If they're on the nightstand, position the crystals on their sides, with the points facing your head. If the crystals are below your bed, have the point facing up, toward your head or your heart. As you become more sensitive, you'll probably have to move the crystals with their points facing away from you. You may even need to move them farther from your bed. Highly sensitive clairsentients sometimes develop insomnia when crystals are too close to their sleeping area.

— *Work with the aroma of pink roses or rose essential oil.* The aroma of pink roses opens the heart chakra, which is the energy center that regulates clairsentience. Keep a pink rose nearby and breathe in its fragrance often. Or, purchase some high-quality essential oil made with real, not synthetic, rose. Put the rose oil over your heart and dab some near your nose where you can frequently enjoy its aroma.

— *Wear a rose quartz necklace.* Just as pink roses open the heart chakra, so does rose quartz crystal. This beautiful pink stone is attuned to the heart chakra. In addition to opening up our clairsentience, rose quartz crystals can help us open to romantic blessings in our life.

— *Increase your sensitivity to physical-touch exercises.* Close your eyes and handle an object on your desk. Touch it slowly and deliberately, noticing the minute details and textures. Rub the item along the back of your hand and your arm, and be aware of the sensations. Have a trusted friend gently blindfold you and hand you unknown items to touch, or food samples to taste. Put all of your awareness on your physical and emotional sensations, and try to guess what each item is.

— *Tune up your body with cardiovascular exercise and light eating.* When we feel tired, heavy, or sluggish, it's more difficult to discern our feelings. Jogging, brisk walking, yoga, or other cardiovascular exercise helps us to more precisely pinpoint the meaning and messages behind our clairsentience. Similarly, eating light, healthful foods keeps us from being weighed down. A sense of heaviness or being stuffed from food can block our awareness of Divine guidance. Anything that can make your body feel better, including a massage, a nap, or a bubble bath, will heighten your sensitivity to your gut feelings.

Protecting Yourself

Clairsentients often complain that they're *too* sensitive. "I absorb the toxic energy of other people's problems," and "I get overwhelmed because I can feel everyone else's emotions," are the two chief complaints among the feeling-oriented set.

Ironically, clairsentients often enter professions that increase their likelihood of physical contact with people. Massage, energy healing, medicine, and counseling are a few common occupations among people who understand the world through their feelings. And while feeling-oriented people are excellent at those professions, they must take measures to ensure that they don't absorb residue from their clients' negative emotions.

There are two ways to deal with this issue: preventive measures and clearing activities. Preventive measures involve shielding yourself from others' toxic energies. Clearing activities involve releasing any toxic energies that you *do* absorb, including those that stem from your own fearful thoughts.

Shielding

Preventive measures are a little like birth control—they're not 100 percent effective, but they do provide considerable protection. There are dozens of ways to shield yourself, and I'm just including my two favorites.

1. Music: While channeling the first part of this book, I was delighted to receive the information in the chapter about music. As you'll recall, the angels said that music acts as a psychic shield, surrounding us with protective energy. In stressful situations, then, it's a good idea to have music continually playing around us.

Music is not only a preventive measure; it's also a clearing measure. Archangel Sandalphon is the Angel of Music, and he works with Archangel Michael to clear away the effects of fear through the use of music. Call upon Sandalphon to help you select the best music in various situations. When you meditate, have music playing, and ask Sandalphon to work with this music to shield and clear you.

2. Pink light: The angels taught me this method one day when I was at the gym. I said hello to a woman I'd never met before, whose path crossed mine on the free-weights floor. She began telling me about her numerous medical operations, in minute detail. I knew that she needed to express herself and wanted a friendly ear. However, I also knew that she was spewing out toxic energy with her endless discourse on illness and disease.

I mentally called upon my angels for help. "*Surround yourself with a tube of pink light,*" they immediately counseled me. I envisioned myself surrounded by a tall cylinder of pink light, as if I were inside a lipstick tube. It extended above my head and below my feet.

"*You've never liked shielding yourself with white light,*" the angels reminded me, "*because you felt like you were isolating yourself from others. Since your life's mission specifically calls for you to interact with others and not to isolate yourself (as you did in your most recent past life), you have shied away from using the white-light shield.*"

Their words were true. Although I knew all about shielding methods, I rarely used them because I wanted to be there for the people I was counseling. I'd once worked with a psychiatrist who counseled people from behind a gigantic oak desk. I'd always thought that he used that desk as a buffer to avoid emotional intimacy with his patients. It was also a power symbol. I didn't want to use white light during my counseling sessions, because it felt like I was isolating myself from my clients.

"*But notice how this pink shield of light is very different. See how it radiates intense Divine love energy out toward this woman.*

Notice, also, how it radiates beautifully strong Divine energy inward toward yourself. And nothing can permeate this pink-light shield but energies that originate from Divine love. So, in this way, you can be fully present for this woman, without taking her illusions of suffering upon yourself."

Since that day, I've been using and teaching the pink-shield technique with great results—and positive feedback from those I've taught it to. Thank you, angels!

Clearing

We sometimes feel tired, irritable, or depressed without knowing why. Often, the culprit stems from our contact with other people's negative mind-sets. If you work in a helping profession, your exposure to toxic emotions is especially high, and it's essential to clear these energies from yourself regularly.

Here are my three favorite clearing methods:

1. Plants: Probably the simplest way to clear yourself of psychic debris is with the help of Mother Nature. Just as plants convert carbon dioxide into fresh oxygen, they also transmute lower energies. Plants are especially helpful in ridding our bodies of energetic toxins.

The angels urge us all to keep a plant next to our bed. A potted plant on the nightstand can do wonders while you sleep! It absorbs the heavy energy that you've ingested during the day, and sends it into the ethers. Don't worry; it won't harm the plant.

If you work with people in any way, but especially as a massage therapist or counselor (where you're open to receiving your clients' released negativity), have plants near your workstation. You'll feel more refreshed at the end of the day by taking this one simple step! The angels say that broad-leafed plants work best, because the wide leaves absorb greater energy fields. So, a pothos or philodendron would be a good choice. Avoid prickly or pointy leaves in the plants that surround you. Interestingly, feng shui, the ancient Chinese art of placement, also recommends avoiding pointy-leafed plants. Apparently, their sword-like leaves don't promote good energy flow.

2. Etheric cord cutting: Anyone who works with other people, either professionally or by offering unpaid acts of kindness, should know about etheric cords and how to handle them. Basically, whenever a person forms a fear-based attachment to you (such as being afraid that you'll leave them, or believing that you are their source of energy or happiness), a cord is constructed between the two of you. This cord is visible to anyone who is clairvoyant, and palpable to anyone who is intuitive.

The cords look like surgical tubing, and they function like gasoline hoses. When a needy person has formed an attachment to you, that person suctions energy from you through this etheric cord. You may not see the cord, but you can feel its effects: namely, you feel tired or sad without knowing why. Well, it's because the person at the other end of the etheric cord has just drawn on your energy, or has just sent you toxic energy through the cord.

So, anytime you've helped someone; or whenever you feel lethargic, sad, or tired, it's a good idea to "cut your cords." You aren't rejecting, abandoning, or divorcing the person by cutting these cords. You're only cutting the dysfunctional, fearful, co-dependent part of the relationship. The loving part of the relationship remains attached.

To cut your own cords, say either mentally or aloud:

"Archangel Michael, I call upon you now.
Please cut the cords of fear that are draining
my energy and vitality. Thank you."

Then, be silent for a few moments. Be sure to inhale and exhale deeply during the process, as breath opens the door for angels to help you. You'll probably feel cords being cut or pulled out of you. You may feel air-pressure changes or other palpable signs that the cord-cutting is occurring.

The people on the other end of the cord will think of you at the moment that their cord is being cut without knowing why. You may even find that you get lots of "just thinking about you" phone messages and e-mails from people who you were "attached" to. Don't buy into faulty thinking about these people. Remember, *you* are not their source of energy or happiness—God is. The cords will grow back each time a person forms a fear-based attachment to you. So, keep cutting your cords as needed.

3. Vacuuming: When we worry about someone, blame ourselves for a person's misery, or massage someone who is in emotional pain, we may take on their negative psychic energy in a misguided form of helpfulness. Everyone does this, especially lightworkers who are ultraconcerned about helping others—often at their own expense. The angels give us methods such as this one to help us stay balanced in our service work. They want us to help others, but not to hurt ourselves in the process. It's a matter of being open to receiving help from others, including the angels. Many lightworkers are wonderful at giving assistance, but not so good at receiving it. This is a method to help counterbalance that tendency.

To vacuum yourself with the help of the angels, mentally

say, "*Archangel Michael, I call upon you now to clear and vacuum the effects of fear.*" You will then mentally see or feel a large angel appear. This is Archangel Michael. He will be accompanied by smaller angels known as the "Band of Mercy."

Notice that Michael is holding a vacuum tube. Watch as he puts that tube in through the top of your head (known as the "crown chakra"). You must decide whether you want the vacuum speed to be on extra-high, high, medium, or low. You will also be directing him where to put the vacuum tube during the clearing process. Mentally direct the vacuum tube inside your head, in your body, and around all of your organs. Vacuum every part, all the way to the tips of your fingers and toes.

You may see or feel clumps of psychic dirt go through the vacuum tube, just like when you're vacuuming a dirty carpet. Any entities that go through the vacuum are humanely treated at the other end by the Band of Mercy, who meets and escorts entities to the Light. Keep vacuuming until no more psychic dirt goes through the tube.

As soon as you're clear, Archangel Michael will reverse the switch so that thick, toothpastelike white light comes out of the tube. This is a form of "caulking" material that will fill in the spaces that formerly held psychic dirt.

The vacuuming technique is one of the most powerful methods that I've ever used. You can also use these methods on other people, in person, or remotely. Just hold the intention of working on them with these methods, and it's done. Even if you don't clearly see or feel anything during the process, or even if you worry, "Am I just making this up?" the results will be palpable. Most people see an immediate lifting of depression and a cessation of anger following a vacuuming session.

Being in Touch with Your Feelings

With practice, you become increasingly tuned in to your feelings, and are more apt to trust their wisdom. If you add to your spiritual repertoire with the power of your thoughts and ideas, you'll have two avenues to receive and follow your Divine guidance. In the next chapter, we'll examine the power of claircognizance, or thoughts from Heaven.

⁓ ⁓ ⁓

How to Recognize and Receive Divine Ideas and Profound Thoughts

When there's some tidbit of knowledge that you know for sure, without knowing *how* you know, it's called *claircognizance,* or "clear knowing." Maybe this has happened to you: You're arguing with a person about a topic that you're only vaguely familiar with, but something deep inside of you tells you a fact or two, and you cling to this knowledge without having evidence to support it. Your companion asks, "But *how* do you know?" And you have no retort but to say, "I just know, that's all."

You've probably been called a "know-it-all" a few times in your life, and this proclamation has a kernel of truth to it. You *do* know a lot, but you're totally puzzled about how you came to own all of this information.

Many great inventors, scientists, authors, futurists, and leaders have used their gift of claircognizance to tap in to the collective unconscious and access new ideas and inspiration. Thomas Edison, for instance, said, "All progress, all success, springs from thinking." It is said that Edison and other great inventors meditate until they receive a brainstorm of inspiration and ideas.

The difference between someone who simply receives such information and someone who also benefits from it is the ability to accept what's happening as something useful and special. So many claircognizants write off their incoming transmissions as information that is glaringly obvious to others. *Everyone knows this stuff,* claircognizants will say to themselves. Then, two years later, they find that the brilliant idea they had conceived has been carried out and marketed by another person. So, the challenge for those who receive their Divine guidance as a thought, idea, or revelation is to accept that this is a unique piece of information that *really could be the answer to their prayer.*

Let's say that you've been praying for Divine guidance to help you leave your job and become self-employed. You then receive an idea for a business that would help others, and this thought comes to you again and again (two characteristics of true Divine guidance). Will you discount the idea, thinking, *Well, everyone dreams of self-employment, so this is obviously pie-in-the-sky wishful thinking?*

I've found that claircognizants benefit from spending time away from the computer and office, and getting a healthy dose of nature and fresh air. Many thinking-oriented people lead work-centered lives, creating a need for balance in the areas of physical fitness, playfulness, family matters, spirituality, and relationships. Even focusing a little extra time on these areas can help a claircognizant feel more clear in following ideas that are borne of the Infinite Mind.

Judgment vs. Discernment

Those who favor a thinking style with regard to angelic communication may have higher Intelligence Quotients (IQs) than average. After all, they're usually avid readers, with a wide range of interests that would land them higher-than-average IQ scores.

A key ingredient in tapping in to that intellectual awareness is being able to differentiate between when you're using discernment versus when you're relying on judgment. There are key differences between these two intellectual behaviors that can determine spiritual outcomes.

Let's start with an example involving cigarette smoking. You're probably aware of the many studies linking smoking to various diseases and health risks. Discernment would say, "I'm not attracted to cigarette smoking or smokers. I don't care for the smell or its effects." Judgment would say, "Smoking is bad. Smokers are bad." Notice the difference? Discernment operates under the "Law of Attraction," which simply asks you to honor your personal preferences without labeling or condemnation.

In a similar vein, when you're unsure of whether or not an idea is Divinely guided, pay attention to your internal mechanisms of discernment. The old adage, "If in doubt, don't," has a lot of wisdom to it. Your inner computer knows if something is off or not. You may not need to reject an entire idea, but you may need to rethink or revise certain components of it.

You may need to seek out experts in areas that are outside of your expertise. If this is the case, mentally ask God and your angels to lead you to these individuals, and you'll delight in seeing how quickly they come to you.

I experienced this phenomenon when I felt that I was supposed to write a book on vegetarianism. I knew that I needed to find a collaborator who was a registered dietitian with a spiritual bent—who was also familiar with vegetarianism. With full faith, I turned my request to find such a person over to God. Three weeks later, at one of my workshops, a registered dietitian named Becky Prelitz introduced herself to me. She had come to see me speak because she was very immersed in spiritual teaching and living. *This is the woman I'm looking for!* I thought to myself. The more I talked to Becky, the more convinced I became that she was the expert who was the answer to my prayer. Today, Becky and her husband, Christopher, are great friends of my husband, Steven, and me; and our book, *Eating in the Light: Making the Switch to Vegetarianism Along the Spiritual Path*, was published by Hay House in 2001.

Common Ways that Claircognizance Occurs

Here are some of the ways in which you may have already received Divine communication through your thought processes:

- You met a new person, and suddenly knew details about him or her without having had previous knowledge of the individual.

- You had knowledge of something related to current events without having read or heard about it.

- You had a premonition of how something (a business venture, a recreational trip, or a relationship, for example) was going to turn out . . . and you were right.

- You had an idea for a business, a book, or an invention that haunted you. You executed the idea and found that it worked out favorably. Or, you ignored it and discovered that someone else with the same idea ran with it and made a fortune.

- You lost your checkbook, keys, or wallet, and when you asked your angels where the item was, you received a sudden knowingness that led you right to it.

True Divine claircognizance is repetitive and positive. It speaks of ways in which you can improve your own life and the lives of others. It is service oriented, and while a certain idea may make you rich and famous, that is a side benefit, and *not* the motivation behind the concept. In fact, it's usually these types of altruistic ideas that lead to benefits for their inventors. Those who pursue self-serving ventures often repel potential clients and customers, who can sense the hollow values behind the idea. My publisher and mentor, Louise L. Hay, once told me that her financial life finally healed when she began focusing on how she could serve, rather than on what she could get. When I applied this same principle to my own life, I found that it had remarkably curative effects on my level of happiness, as well as on my career and income.

You might say that true claircognizance helps you "build a better mousetrap," or do something that will truly help others, in such a way that will inspire people to seek you out as a customer, client, sponsor, audience member, publisher, and so forth. This force comes from the Creator, Who knows of your true talents, passions, and interests, and Who knows how these characteristics can be used to help others. In Biblical times, money was referred to as "talents," and *you* have talents that you can exchange for money.

True claircognizance doesn't just wave a dream under your nose and then taunt you to discover how to manifest it. No! It gives you complete step-by-step instructions. The trick, though, is to remember that God only teaches you one step at a time. You receive this information in the form of repetitive thoughts (or feelings, visions, or words, depending upon your spiritual orientation) that tell you to *do something*. The "something" usually seems insignificant: Call this person, write this letter, attend this meeting, read this book, for example. If you follow the instructions and complete Step A, then in the same repetitive manner, you're given the next set of instructions for Step B. Step by step, God guides you all the way to the realization of your intended manifestation.

You always have free will, so you can ignore the guidance anytime you choose. However, most people find that if they don't complete one of the Divinely guided steps, they feel stuck, like they're spinning their wheels in the mud. I always ask people who tell me that they feel blocked, "What piece of Divine guidance have you been repetitively receiving but are ignoring?" Always, I find that this guidance (which they're avoiding because of some fear of making a life change) is the key ingredient they've been searching for.

Angels give you ideas in response to your prayers for guidance. You receive this Divine guidance at moments when your mind is receptive, such as during dreamtime, meditation, exercise, or even while watching a TV program or movie (when your mind tends to go on cruise control). You'll feel excited and energized by Divinely guided ideas, and it's important not to counteract these ideas with pessimistic thoughts. The idea rings true, and you'll know—deep in your soul—that this is it! Sure, any idea can fail. *But it can also succeed!* And trying is what gives your life meaning at the end of the day.

If you've had some negative experiences with respect to following hunches in the past, you may understandably feel gun-shy now. You may have decided to play it safe and secure by avoiding major life changes. That's fine, as long as you're happy with your current circumstances! But if there's an area of your life that's off-balance, it's natural for you (as well as God and the angels) to want to heal the situation. That's called achieving "homeostasis," which is the instinctual drive to achieve balance that is common to all living things.

Skepticism, Pragmatism, and Faith

More than anything, though, claircognizants sometimes waver when it comes to faith. When you're a thinker, it's easy to think yourself into a box of skepticism. Faith seems illogical, and it rests upon so many intangible factors.

Yet a good scientist always experiments before drawing a conclusion. Whether your hypothesis is geared in favor of believing in angels or not, take the time to put your hypothesis to a test. For instance, God and the angels hear our thoughts (don't worry—they don't judge them), so you can call upon Heaven without eliciting raised eyebrows from your colleagues. Mentally ask your angels to help you with some area of your personal or professional life.

Then, notice what help comes to you after you've made your

request. It may be an instant response, where you have a strong impulse or idea, or it may come in a more tangible fashion, where a person will "just happen" to hand you a journal article with the information you seek. The two key ingredients in this experiment are (1) *asking* for help (the Law of Free Will prevents Heaven from helping, without us giving permission); and (2) *noticing* the help that's being received.

Being aware of this type of assistance is entirely different from holding a forced scavenger hunt where you're seeking clues. False guidance is always the product of struggle and worry. True Divine guidance always comes easily on natural wings of love.

I find that most claircognizant people have had experiences with their deceased loved ones in which they knew that their grandparent, parent, or another beloved person was with them. Without actually seeing or feeling that deceased person's presence, the claircognizant had a *knowingness* of the loved one's proximity.

This same sort of knowingness creates other psychic hits for claircognizants in areas related to careers, family, and health. Without knowing how they know, the claircognizant receives incoming information that is both accurate and helpful. The more you can learn to trust and follow that information, the more you will benefit from your internal guidance system.

For instance, you may get an idea about opening a new business. The idea is foolproof, and you wonder why you never thought of it before. You venture forward, and all the doors open for you: financing, location, partnerships, and more. The business is a rapid success, and you know that you were guided by true Divine wisdom.

The Spiritual Mentorship Program

There are many beings in Heaven who would like to help you, and not all of them are your guardian angels. Some of them are ordinary people who have passed on and who have a strong desire to teach and help those of us who are living. Many of these people are extremely talented and accomplished, and they form what is known as the "Spiritual Mentorship Program."

On Earth, a mentor is an accomplished person in your chosen field who shows you the ropes and gives you advice, guidance, and introductions. The Spiritual Mentorship Program is similar, in that you're assigned to an expert who spends time guiding you through the process related to your chosen vocation or avocation.

You can work with any famous deceased person, or any unknown-but-great person in the spirit world. Most of them are very happy to pass along their knowledge. It gives them a sense of meaning to help others, in the same way that you enjoy performing service work. And, there's no charge for their services, so you can meet with them in your own home—wearing your pajamas!

When I first felt guided to contact a mentor, I chose a specific author whom I greatly admire (he won't allow me to divulge his name because he feels that would only give glory to his ego-personality). So I mentally asked him to help me write the book *The Lightworker's Way*. Immediately, he came to me. Although I could only faintly see him, I sensed his presence on a feeling, knowing, and hearing level quite strongly.

I was so surprised that this author actually came to visit me (I was starstruck!) that I didn't know what to say. I stammered, "You . . . you . . . you're here!"

The author then said to me, "You're obviously not prepared. Please call me when you're better prepared to work with me."

At that time, I was just beginning to give psychic readings to famous people whom I highly respected. I noticed that my admiration of their work made me feel intimidated by them. I would act differently around these so-called celebrities than I would around "regular" people. This bugged me, because I knew this was an ego issue. It meant that I saw famous people as being "above" me, or in other words, as being separated from me.

So, I asked Jesus and the archangels to come into my dreams and clear away any ego issues that made me think that anyone was either above me or below me. As always, this request worked immediately! In the morning, I felt a shift. I can't tell you *how* it happened. I can just tell you that it *did* happen. From that point forward, I didn't feel intimidated by people whom I admired.

Since that time, I've called upon additional mentors to help me. One time, I was jogging and experienced terrible pain in the side of my stomach (known as "side stitches"). I immediately asked for help, and was pleasantly surprised when a man in the spirit world came to help me whom I recognized as Jim Fixx, the late author of *The Complete Book of Running*. He told me to concentrate on keeping the top of my head level while running, instead of my bouncy head-bobbing running style. This meant extending the length and smoothness of each running stride. When I stopped bouncing my head up and down, my side stitches went away, and I haven't had any recurrences. Jim also helps me with endurance and speed while running.

I've taught many audience members about the Spiritual Mentorship Program, and the majority of them have successfully "adopted" a mentor in Heaven. Some of these mentors are famous inventors, writers, healers, and musicians who have passed on. For instance, a pre-med student in Chicago writes letters to Albert Einstein and receives guidance, a songwriter in Atlanta corresponds with John Denver using automatic writing, and an architect in the Midwest talks with Michelangelo for inspiration.

To engage in the Spiritual Mentorship Program, simply think about a being with whom you would like to correspond. If you can't think of anyone specifically, ask God and the angels to assign a person to you who is an expert in a specific area (just as I did when I was running).

Then, even if you can't hear, see, or feel the presence of your new mentor, ask the person a question anyway. Either write this question down on paper, type it on a computer or typewriter, think the question, or say it aloud. The mentor will hear your question, regardless of how you ask it.

Notice the answers that come to you as thoughts, words, feelings, or visions. It's a good idea to write the questions and answers down, like in an interview. A full explanation of how to engage in "automatic writing" is on page 223.

Whether you believe that these messages from your spiritual mentors are literal or figurative, you'll find that writing down your questions, and then writing the answers that you receive as thoughts, words, feelings, or visions, opens you up to new ideas and creative insights.

How to Increase Your Claircognizance

Since claircognizance can come about subtly, as a thought or an idea, it's easy to miss this high-level method through which Heaven communicates with us. You might dismiss your Divinely inspired thought or idea without recognizing it as an answer to your prayers. You might mistake it for an idle thought or a daydream instead of Heaven's inspiration.

Claircognizants also ignore their Divine guidance because they believe that what they know is obvious to others. "Everybody knows that!" a claircognizant will decide, and won't capitalize upon the brilliant idea that they just received. It doesn't help that many claircognizants have been teased for being know-it-alls, so they hesitate to speak up for fear of being ridiculed. Yet, their know-it-all label has a kernel of truth to it, for claircognizants are very tapped in to the collective unconscious.

So, it's important to really pay attention to your thoughts and ideas. That includes the repetitive thoughts and also the novel ideas. Divine guidance comes both as thoughts that hammer away at you repeatedly with suggestions, and also as lightning-bulb-type inspirations. One of the best ways to pay attention to this form of guidance is to keep a daily journal in which you have a conversation with yourself about your thoughts and ideas. The journal format could be like an interview with your higher self, perhaps set up in a question-and-answer format. In this way, you can more easily bring unconscious information to your awareness.

When you get a thought, don't second-guess yourself. Instead, give your thoughts and ideas a moment to speak up. Ask the thoughts and ideas, "What do you want to tell me?" It could be an insight such as, "This new person I've just been introduced to doesn't seem honorable." Or, it could be an inspired idea that helps you *know* for the truth of a spiritual principle, or a walloping idea for a can't-miss new business.

By keeping a journal, you can assess the patterns and accuracy of your thoughts and ideas. You'll get in the habit of gaining awareness about which thoughts are truly Divinely inspired. You've probably had the experience of ignoring your thoughts and saying later, "I *knew* that was going to happen!" or "I *knew* I shouldn't have gone there!" Our successes and mistakes both teach us to trust and follow our insights.

I also find that many people who are thinking oriented (as opposed to feeling, visual, or auditory oriented) tend to be workaholics. They often hole up in their offices, strapped to the chairs in front of their computers. All of this work is fine, as long as it's balanced with time spent outdoors. Yet I usually have to urge claircognizants to go out in nature. It's foreign to their comfort zones!

Once outside, though, claircognizants find that the fresh air, plants, and trees help to sharpen their psychic senses. They become even more open to, and aware of, their Divine inspiration. The peace of the outdoors makes it easier to hear one's thoughts and to take note of clever ideas. As we take time for personal time-outs, we take a break from the world of clocks and telephones. We become more tuned in to the inner rhythm of our bodies—and all of nature. Among other benefits, spending regular time outdoors helps us develop "good timing," which really means that we notice and follow the rhythm of life. When we return to the office, we've developed more acute instincts with respect to the best time to make that phone call, send that e-mail, or speak up at that meeting. Our time outdoors might also inspire us to break away from the office completely, and forge a career that matches our heart's desire more fully.

True and False Claircognizance

Some people are skeptical about following their intuition because they've done so in the past and have been burned as a result. Perhaps you had a great idea one time, but when you followed through on it, everything turned into a mess. So you're reluctant to ever trust your ideas again.

Usually, these situations involve two types of patterns:

1. Your initial idea was Divinely inspired, but then fear took you off the path. When you initially received the idea, it was based upon true Divine guidance, which always stems from love. But somewhere along the way, you got scared. This fear blocked your receptivity to continued guidance and creative ideas, took you off of your original inspired path, and triggered behavior and decisions that originated from the ego. When we partner with our egos, unhappiness and errors inevitably follow.

For instance, a woman I know named Bernice had a wonderful idea to start a home-based business as a personal fitness trainer. The idea seemed perfect, as it was a service that would help others in a field that she enjoyed, and it would allow her to stay home with her toddler while earning some money. So, Bernice quit her day job and opened the business at her home. The first month, five people signed up as clients, which provided Bernice with enough money to pay her bills plus have extra money left over.

Yet, Bernice worried whether her initial success would continue. *Where would her new clients come from?* she worried. After ruminating about her future for several days, Bernice decided to purchase advertising in several newspapers. She also bought full-color brochures, with matching stationery and business cards. Her expenses for these investments were high, but Bernice decided that she needed to "spend money to make money."

The next month, Bernice only signed up one new client. She worried even more about her business, and spent additional money on advertising. But nothing that she tried seemed to work, and within four months, Bernice decided to return to her previous job to ensure that she'd bring in a steady income.

What happened? she wondered. In reviewing her situation, we find that Bernice truly did receive Divine guidance in starting her business. This was reinforced by her initial success, which gave her enough money to pay her bills, with a surplus afterward. It was only when Bernice started to let fear creep into the picture that things started to dry up. That's also when she started forcing things to happen, through misguided advertising and unnecessary purchases. Her expenses went up and her income went down because she began listening to her ego's fears instead of her higher self's reassurance and guidance.

2. *Instead of acknowledging your Divine guidance, you forced something to happen, or you listened to someone else's opinion and ignored your inner teacher.* Sometimes we want to hear what we want to hear, so we'll decide that "he's the guy," even if our intuition (and best friends) are screaming that he's not right for us. Or, we'll decide that God wants us to quit our job and move to Sedona, Arizona, when our gut feelings urge us to make a gradual career transition. In some cases, we'll betray our intuition and do something that's against our better judgment, because a strong-willed person will talk us into something.

True and False Claircognizant Guidance

So, how *do* we know if an idea is God-inspired brilliance, or a route to a wild goose chase? The chapter called "How to Know If It's Truly Your Angels or Just Your Imagination" (page 149), lists distinctions between true and false guidance. With regard to thoughts, ideas, and revelations, the characteristics to notice are:

— *Consistency.* True guidance is repetitive, and the idea will stick with you over time. Although it may build in detail and application, the core idea will stay the same. False guidance changes its course and structure constantly.

— *Motivation.* True guidance is motivated by a desire to improve a situation. False guidance's chief motivation is to make you rich and famous. Although true guidance may yield those rewards, they are side benefits, and not the central motivation for the idea.

— *Tone.* True guidance is uplifting, motivating, and encouraging. It urges you on, saying, "You can do it!" False guidance is the opposite, shredding your confidence to pieces.

— *Origination.* True guidance appears quickly, like a lightning bolt, in response to prayer or meditation. False guidance comes slowly, in response to worry. When you get an idea, back up and examine the trail of thoughts preceding it. If you were worrying about something, your ego may have conjured up a scheme to rescue you. If you were meditating peacefully, however, your higher self had the room to truly connect with the Divine collective unconscious and has probably handed you a gem of an idea.

— *Familiarity.* An idea that comes from true Divine guidance usually fits in with your natural inclinations, talents, passions, and interests. False guidance usually contains "left-field," advice, involving activities that hold no interest for you.

By noticing these characteristics, you can increase your confidence in the ideas that you follow. You'll know that you're on the right path, and you'll use all of your higher intentions to create success. A healthy confidence level correlates to holding clear, laser-focused thoughts that lead to rapid manifestation.

If you combine your claircognizance with the ability to hear the voice of the Divine, as we'll discuss in the next section, you'll take your idea-manufacturing process to an even higher level.

How to Hear Your Angels

I think it's ironic that I, a former psychotherapist who once worked in locked hospital psychiatric wards, now teach people how to hear voices! Yet when we listen for the voice of God and the angels, it's the sanest sound we can ever hear. Their voice can show us love in the face of seeming chaos, and provide us with logical solutions when challenges arise. Hearing the voice of Spirit is called *clairaudience,* or "clear hearing." In this chapter, we'll discuss what clairaudience is, and how to increase its volume and clarity.

Common Ways That We Hear Heaven's Voice

Chances are excellent that you've heard your angels and other spiritual beings speak to you throughout your life. Have any of the following situations happened to you?

- Upon awakening, you hear your name called by a disembodied voice.

- Out of nowhere, you hear a strain of beautiful, celestial-sounding music.

- You repeatedly hear a song, either in your head or on the radio.

- You hear a loud, shrill ringing sound in one ear.

- You overhear a conversation in which a stranger says the exact thing that you need to hear.

- You just "happen" to turn on the TV or radio at the exact moment that a relevant discussion is occurring.

- You hear a deceased loved one's voice, in your mind, in a dream, or outside of your head.

- You hear the disembodied voice of a living loved one, and it turns out that they needed assistance just then.

- You hear the telephone or the doorbell ring. No one is there, but you can sense that your deceased loved one is trying to get your attention.

- A disembodied voice gives you a warning or a life-enhancing message.

- You're looking for a lost item, you pray for assistance, and then you hear a voice tell you where to locate the item.

Answers Come in Response to Questions

God and the angels speak to us in response to our queries. So, we can kick-start a conversation simply by directing a question to them.

One time, I wanted to know why certain Christian factions

promoted the idea that it was beneficial to "fear God." I just couldn't understand why anyone would fear our loving God, nor why anyone would *aspire* to fear Him. So, I asked my angels to help me understand this belief system. I had no sooner asked the question than I was scanning the stations on my car radio. The scanner stopped on a Christian talk show, and at that very moment, the host began explaining why Christians "should" fear God. I didn't agree with his message, but I was very grateful to hear the answer to my question . . . especially so quickly after asking.

Is there a question that you have, or some area of your life in which you desire guidance? Take a moment right now and mentally ask God and the angels your question. Hold the intention of giving that question to Heaven, and trust that you will receive an answer. Even if you can't hear Heaven answering you right now, be assured that Heaven can definitely hear you!

You should receive an auditory response to your question within a day or so. Sometimes you'll hear the answer in the form of a song. You may notice a tune playing repeatedly on the radio or in your mind. The answer to your question could be in the song's lyrics. Or, if the song reminds you of someone, it could be a message that this person (living or deceased) is thinking about you.

Usually, when we hear our voice called out in the morning, it means that our angels or guides simply want to say hello to us. It's easiest for them to deliver this greeting when we're just waking up, because our lucid mind is more open to spiritual communications. We're also more apt to remember the message when half-awake, as opposed to being fully asleep. If they have another message to add to their greeting, they will specify that message to us at the same time. So, don't worry that you've heard your name called and that someone wants to get through to you. It's simply a loving greeting to let you know that you're being watched over.

If, after asking Heaven a question, you don't receive a reply, it could be that you've overlooked it, or maybe you don't want to hear the message that Heaven is sending you because you didn't appreciate the guidance you were given at some time in the past, so you block yourself from hearing it. Keep asking the question until you hear the answer. Ask your angels to help you to hear, and it will happen eventually.

A spiritual-counseling student of mine named Tienna was frustrated because she'd been in my psychic-development course for three days and still hadn't heard from her angels. Tienna complained that during her angel readings, she only heard staccato, one- or two-word messages. For instance, she was giving a reading to a classmate and heard the words *uncle* and *car accident* in her ear. Well, it turned out that Tienna's classmate had lost an uncle in a car accident.

"But I want to hear more than just one or two words!" Tienna complained. "I want to have full-on conversations with God and the angels."

I asked Tienna's angels for help, and I heard them say to her, "Just stay in the class, Tienna. With persistence and patience, you will hear us soon." I relayed that message to Tienna.

By the fifth day of our spiritual-counseling class, Tienna bounded up to me excitedly. "I hear them, I hear them!" she exclaimed. Tienna had a clairaudient breakthrough in exactly the way that her angels had predicted: through persistent intention to hear, and through patience in surrendering "when" that would happen. From that day forward, Tienna had full-blown auditory discussions with her angels, who gave her both personal guidance, and information for her clients.

Ringing in the Ears

Most lightworkers report hearing a high-pitched ringing sound in one ear. It's a shrill noise that can be painful and intrusive. When checked by a physician, tinnitus (a disturbance of the auditory nerve) is usually ruled out. That's because the ringing is of a nonphysical origin.

The ringing is a band of woven information, encoded in electrical impulses. Heaven downloads guidance, assistance, and information through this bandwidth. It sounds like a computer modem hooking into the Internet.

Sometimes the ringing is accompanied by a pinching or pulling sensation on the earlobe. This happens when the angels and guides especially want our attention. You don't need to consciously understand the message encoded within the ringing sound. You just need to commit to receiving it. The information will be stored in your unconscious, where it will positively influence your actions, ensuring that you don't procrastinate with respect to your lightworker mission.

Please don't worry that the ringing could be coming from a lower or dark source. The ringing shows that the energetic frequency of the encoded information comes from a high place of Divine love. Lower forces wouldn't be able to work with such a high frequency.

The ringing sound is actually an answer to your prayers for guidance about your life's mission. If it becomes too loud, painful, or intrusive, mentally tell your angels that the ringing sound is hurting you, and ask them to turn down the volume. The information will still be transmitted to you; it just will come to you in a quieter fashion. If the earlobe pinching or pulling becomes painful, tell your angels and guides about the pain, and ask them to stop.

When I requested that my angels and guides turn down the volume of the ringing and to stop hurting me with earlobe pinching, I was never again bothered by loud ringing or painful ears. The angels certainly aren't offended by our requests. They need our feedback so that they best know how to help us.

How Do I Know Who's Talking to Me?

If you're concerned about the true identity of a voice that's speaking to you, simply ask your caller to identify him- or herself. If you don't believe or trust the answer that you receive, ask the spiritual being to prove their identity to you. As you'll discover, the being will say or do something that will stir beautiful emotions within you; or will be something that only that particular being could do or say. Here are some guidelines:

- God's voice sounds very loud, male, to-the-point, friendly, and casual, with good humor and modern vernacular.

- The archangels sound very loud, male, to-the-point, formal, and direct. They speak a lot about Divine love; about getting on track with our mission; and overcoming doubts, fears, and procrastination with respect to our mission.

- The angels sound almost Shakespearean at times, with very archaic and formal speech patterns.

- Our deceased loved ones sound just like they did when they were living, although their voice may sound stronger and younger. They will use the same vocabulary and speaking style that they did when they were physically alive.

- Our higher self sounds like our own voice.

- The ego sounds abusive, discouraging, paranoid, depressing, and begins sentences with the word *I* because it is egocentric.

How to Increase Your Clairaudience

We're all naturally psychic, and that includes clairaudience and all of the other "clairs." We usually find, however, that each person possesses one primary channel of Divine communication. Some people are naturally auditory, and the first thing they observe when they meet someone new is the sound of that person's voice. Some people are naturally visual, and the first thing they notice in new acquaintances is that person's appearance, including their movements and actions. Those who are naturally feeling oriented notice how new people make them feel, whether that new person touches them, and even how the fabric of their clothing feels. Thinking-oriented individuals are aware of whether a new person is interesting, intelligent, potentially helpful in their career, or logical.

If you're naturally auditory, you already hear the voice of God and your angels. However, if this isn't your primary channel of Divine communication, you may struggle to hear Heaven's voice. You may read about accounts of people who hear warnings or messages from their angels, and wonder, *Why don't my angels talk to me?* Here are several methods that can help you hear the voice of the Divine, loud and clear:

— *Clearing the ear chakras:* Each of the psychic senses is governed by a chakra energy center. As we've discussed, clairsentience (feeling) is regulated by the heart chakra; claircognizance (thinking) is connected to the crown chakra; clairaudience (hearing) is governed by the two ear chakras; and the next chapter will talk about the third eye's connection to clairvoyance (seeing).

The ear chakras are located above the eyebrows, inside the head. They appear to be a violet-red color. Imagine two violet-red disks spinning clockwise above your eyebrows. See or feel an image of sending them beams of cleansing white light. See or feel this white light illuminating the ear chakras from the inside. Notice how clean and large the ear chakras are becoming. Repeat this method daily, or whenever you feel that your psychic hearing is clogged.

— *Releasing psychic debris:* If you've been verbally abused by others or by your own self-deprecating talk, your ear chakras are probably clogged with toxins from the negative words directed toward you. Mentally ask your angels to surround you with comforting energy. You can release the pent-up negativity in your ear chakras by writing down the names of those who have verbally abused you (including yourself) and putting the paper in a plastic container of water. Then, put this container into the freezer compartment of your refrigerator. You'll have an immediate sense of release as you put these names in the freezer. Keep them in the freezer for a minimum of three months. (By the way, this is a wonderful method of releasing *any* kind of problem.)

— *Reopening tuned-out frequencies:* When you were a kid, did you tune out the voice of your mom, your dad, your teacher, or some other person—including yourself? As a child, your ability to shut out incessant nagging or other verbal unpleasantries may have been your only available defense mechanism. The trouble is, though, you may have tuned out *all* the other voices in the frequency range of those you originally tuned out. So, you may have difficulty hearing a Heavenly voice that is in the same pitch or tone of your mother, for instance. You might not hear your higher self's voice if you tuned your own voice out long ago. Fortunately, you can simply "change your mind" to reopen your physical and spiritual ears to the full range of frequencies. Since your firm intention to shut out sound was the origination of the blockage, simply make a different firm intention to now hear all ranges of sound frequencies.

— *Increasing sensitivity to sound:* Take time each day to notice the sounds around you. Tune in to the sound of birds singing, children laughing, and cars driving by, for instance.

Also, notice the sounds that accompany ordinary behaviors, such as turning the pages of a book, writing a note, or breathing. By paying attention to subtle and not-so-subtle sounds in your environment, you heighten your sensitivity to the voices of the angels and your guides.

— *Protecting your physical ears:* As your sensitivity to the sound frequency of the angels increases, you'll find that loud noises will bother you more than they did before. You'll need to cover your ears when you're in an airplane that's landing, and avoid front-row seats at loud rock concerts, for instance. You'll also need to ask friends to speak more quietly to you on the telephone, request restaurant tables that are far away from noisy groups of people, and secure hotel rooms positioned far from the elevator and ice machines.

— *Asking your angels:* Some people have quiet angels and introverted spirit guides. Just like when you're having a conversation with a living person, don't be afraid to ask whomever you're conversing with, "Would you please speak a little louder?" Our celestial friends really want to communicate with us, and they need our honest feedback to help guide them in knowing the best way to make their voices heard. My mother, Joan Hannan, was having difficulty hearing her angels and guides, so she asked them to speak louder. But she still couldn't hear them, so Mom said in a powerful voice, "Please, speak even louder." She then heard her grandmother's voice say very loudly, "I'm right here!" My great-grandmother seemed to mean, "You don't have to yell; I'm standing right next to you. I can hear you just fine!"

You're always in control of your Divine communication, and if you want Heaven to turn down the volume or intensity of your auditory messages, just ask. In the next chapter, we'll explore the world of clairvoyance, and look at ways to help you see angels and Heaven-sent messages.

❧ How to See Your Angels ☙

The angels wish to connect with you visually, as much or more than you wish to connect with them. They're helping us communicate with them by making their presence clearly known. My books *Angel Visions* and *Angel Visions II* (both published by Hay House) contain dozens of stories about people who have had contact with angels.

What It's Like to See Angels

Many of my psychic-development students mistakenly believe that clairvoyance means seeing angels as clear, opaque figures who look as solidly three-dimensional as living humans. They expect their visions to be outside of their head, instead of a mental image in their mind's eye.

However, most examples of clairvoyance are similar to the mental pictures you see in your mind when you're daydreaming or having a nocturnal dream. Just because the image is in your mind's eye doesn't make the vision less real or valid. When I explain this to my students, they often exclaim, "Oh, so I am seeing angels after all!"

With clear intention and practice, most people can develop the ability to see angels outside their mental sphere with their eyes open. In other words, you'll look at a person and see an angel clearly hovering over that person's shoulders. But beginning clairvoyants usually must close their physical eyes while "scanning" a person. Then, in their mind's eye, the beginning clairvoyant sees images of that person's guardian angels.

Some people see lights or colors in the beginning stages of their clairvoyance. Others see fleeting visions of an angel's head or wings. Some individuals see the angels as translucent and colorless; or opalescent, with shimmering colors radiating from them. Still others see angels as full-figured beings, complete with brightly colored hair and clothing.

During stressful times or following intense prayer, some people will have vivid angel encounters, similar to an apparition experience. With their eyes wide open and while fully awake, the person sees an angel. That angel may look like a human being, or may take on a traditional angelic image, with a gown and wings. The angel is clearly there. The person may even touch or hear the angel and not realize that it's a non-human until after the angel disappears.

Photography Orbs

One of the newest ways in which angels are showing themselves to us is by appearing on photographs as "orbs of light." If you wish to see evidence of angelic beings, you can now capture them on film! Their images appear as globes of white light when the photos are developed.

The best way to photograph these orbs is by taking a picture of a newborn baby or a spiritually minded person. Or, try taking photographs when you're at a metaphysically related workshop, especially when the topic is "angels." You will find dozens of these orbs when the photos are developed. This method works best when you hold the intention of seeing the angels while you're taking the photos. Mentally ask the angels to appear on film as you snap the pictures.

Other Angel Visions

Other ways in which we see the angels include:

— *Dreams.* Dr. Ian Stevenson of the University of Virginia has catalogued thousands of cases of "dream visitations," in which people have interacted with their deceased loved ones or angels during a dream. Dr. Stevenson says that "degree of vividness" is the characteristic that distinguishes mere dreams from true visitations.[1] That would include vivid colors, intense emotions, and a more-than-real feeling to the dream. When you awaken from a dream visitation, the experience stays with you longer than an ordinary dream. You may remember explicit details about a dream visitation many years after it occurs.

— *Angel lights.* Seeing sparkles or flashes of light indicates that angels are nearby. You're seeing the energy sparks as the angels move across your field of vision. This effect is similar to seeing sparks from the back of a car. It's simply friction, and it means that your spiritual sight is adjusted to seeing energy waves. About half of my audience members around the world report seeing these sparkles and light flashes on a regular basis. Many people are reluctant to publicly admit seeing these lights for fear that they're hallucinating. They're not. Seeing angel lights is a very real—and normal—experience.

— *Colored mists.* Seeing a green, purple, or other-colored mist is a sign that you're in the presence of angels.

— *Angel clouds.* Looking up in the sky and noticing a cloud in the shape of an angel is another way that the angels let us know that they're with us.

— *Seeing signs.* Finding a feather, a coin, a stopped clock, moved objects in your home, lights flickering, or other visual oddities let you know that an angel is saying, "Hello, I'm here" to you. Deceased loved ones often make their presence known by sending birds, butterflies, moths, or specific flowers to you.

— *Seeing a vision.* Seeing a mental movie that provides you with true information about a person or situation, or that gives you guidance about your life purpose or making changes, is a sign of being in the presence of angels. So is glimpsing a brief image of something symbolic. For example, when I meet a health-care worker, I invariably "see" a nurse's cap over that person's head. The angels often send this information to us—especially when we're striving to make the world a better place.

Seven Steps to Opening Your Third Eye

An energy center between our two physical eyes, known as the "Third-Eye Chakra," regulates the amount and intensity of our clairvoyance. Opening the third eye is an essential component of seeing across the veil into the spirit world.

Here are the seven steps to opening your third-eye chakra:

1. First affirm to yourself, "It's safe for me to see." Say this affirmation repeatedly, and if you sense any tension or fear while saying it, breathe deeply. With each exhalation, imagine blowing out your fears about being clairvoyant (more on releasing fears follows this section).

2. Take a clear quartz crystal and hold it in your dominant hand (the hand that you favor when writing). Imagine a beam of

white light coming from above and going into your crystal. Hold the intention that this white light is now clearing your crystal of any negativity it may have absorbed.

3.   Hold that clear quartz crystal, still in your dominant hand, just slightly above the space that is in between your two eyebrows. Move your middle finger so that it's pointing through the crystal toward your third eye (which is between your two physical eyes, and slightly above your eyebrows).

4.   Then take your nondominant hand (the hand you normally don't write with) and place the middle finger of that hand at the highest point on the *back* (not the top) of your head.

5.   Imagine a powerful and bright lightning bolt coming from your dominant hand's middle finger. The lightning bolt goes through your third eye and then ends up at your nondominant hand's middle finger. You're making a battery circuit, with your dominant hand sending energy and your nondominant hand receiving the energy. As the energy runs through your head, it's clearing away psychic debris and awakening your third eye. This process normally takes one to two minutes, and you may feel some pressure in your head, warmth in your fingers, and tingling in your hands. Those are normal sensations from the energy work involved.

6.   Next, put your right hand above your right ear, still holding the crystal in your dominant hand. Do the same thing with your left hand above your left ear. Imagine white light coming out of your dominant hand's middle finger. Slowly move both hands simultaneously toward the highest part of the *back* of your head. Repeat this seven times in a sweeping motion. Hold the

intention of hooking the back of your third eye (which looks just like the back of a physical eye) to the occipital lobe at the back of your head. The occipital lobe is the area of the brain that registers awareness and recognition of your visions. It looks like a thin, round skullcap that you're wearing angled on the back of your head.

With the white light, you're excavating a huge, five-inch chamber extending from the back of your third eye all the way to your occipital lobe. This chamber connects the flow of vision from your third eye to the visual part of your brain. In this way, you'll be more aware of the visions that you have, and you'll also understand their meaning. I've worked with many people who had clean, open third eyes, yet they complained of having no, or limited, clairvoyance. *Having a clean, open third eye is not enough to ensure clairvoyance!* Without the connection between the third eye and the occipital lobe, a person wouldn't be aware of, or understand, their visions. It's like showing a movie without having the projector light on.

7. The final step is to put the middle finger of your dominant hand on top of the crystal, over your third eye (slightly above the area between your two physical eyes). You're going to lift any shields that you may have put over your third eye. With feathery, upward stroking movements, coax the shield to lift, like you're opening a window blind. Be sure to breathe while you're performing this step. Holding your breath will slow the process. Repeat the shield-lifting at least seven times, or until you sense that any shields are lifted.

You can also perform this process on another person. If you know someone who is spiritual and open-minded, especially someone who has experience performing energy healings, have them conduct this process on you. While these seven steps can be self-administered, their power is amplified when another person with clear intention (meaning a minimum of skepticism) performs them on you.

After you, or another person, administer these seven steps, you should notice a marked improvement in your mental visions. When you close your eyes and imagine a garden, you will probably see stronger and more vivid colors and pictures than you did before the procedure. Your nighttime dreams may become more vivid and memorable, and your photographic memory will most likely increase.

Again, the images you see may not appear as something outside of yourself. The mental movies may play on a screen that's inside your head. With practice, you'll be able to project and see those images outwardly. However, whether the visions are in your mind's eye or external is irrelevant. I find that my psychic accuracy is identical whether it's a mental image or something that I see outside of my head. The location of the vision isn't important. What matters is that you notice and give attention to the images, because they're so often visual messages from our angels.

Healing the Fear Blocks to Clairvoyance

If, after going through the seven-step procedure, you still find that your mental pictures are lesser in size, clarity, or color than you desire, then you probably have some fears blocking you. These fears are entirely normal, and they can be readily cured whenever you're ready.

For instance, you may be afraid of:

1. Losing control

- *The fear:* You may worry that if you open your clairvoyance, you'll be overwhelmed with visions of angels and dead people everywhere you go. You may also fear that God will try to control you, or make unacceptable plans for you.

- *The truth:* Clairvoyance is like a television set that you can turn on, off, or dim as you wish. And God's will for you is identical to your higher self's will for yourself. The Big Plan has lots of happiness and plentitude in store for you, plus you'll find greater meaning in all areas of your life.

2. Seeing something spooky

- *The fear:* You can't stand haunted houses or monster movies, and you don't want to see anything smacking of ghouls or goblins floating around your home.

- *The truth:* If you've been able to watch the movie *The Sixth Sense* with your eyes open, you've seen the worst. The spirit world is beautiful, something that Hollywood hasn't caught on to yet. Even the Earthbound spirits and fear thought-forms (the so-called fallen angels) aren't half as bad as the average big-screen renditions of life-after-death. Most deceased people look radiant, youthful, and exude happiness. Wouldn't you look wonderful if you knew you never again had to pay another bill?

3. Being fooled

- *The fear:* "What if it's my imagination and I'm just making it all up?" Or, worse, "What if I'm contacted by lower-world spirits who are posing as my guardian angels?"

- *The truth:* The reason why studies show that children have the most verifiable psychic experiences is because they don't get hung up on worrying whether or not it's their imagination. Joan of Arc is quoted as saying to her inquisitors, who asked her if she was imagining hearing the voice of God, "How else would God speak to me, if not through my imagination?" In other words, just because it's our imagination doesn't mean it isn't real, valid, or accurate.

Sometimes, I'm asked, "Aren't you worried about being fooled by a demon masquerading as an angel?" This question implies that demons shop at costume stores, drape themselves in white feathers, and—boom!—wrap us around their claw-tipped fingers. The fact is that there *are* lower-world energies and beings whom I wouldn't invite to my home for dinner, just like there are living people whom I choose not to hang out with. But this is no reason to shield yourself from seeing clairvoyantly.

I mean, if I asked you if you'd rather walk down a dark alley on the wrong side of town at midnight or high noon, of course you'd say noon, right? And the reason? So that you can *see* who's there, of course. Well, the same holds true for the spirit world. Since those unsavory beings are there anyway, wouldn't you rather be able to see who the players are so that you can call upon Archangel Michael to act as a "bouncer" at your home's front door, ensuring that no one gets through without proper I.D.—and identifying them as a being of high integrity and a big inner light?

The inner light is the best indicator of a being's integrity, whether they're a living person or someone in the spirit world. With clairsentience, you can sense a person's character; with claircognizance, you just know that someone is of high integrity or not; and with clairvoyance, you can literally see the glowing light within.

So-called fallen beings in the spirit world can't mimic the huge glowing light that emanates from the belly and radiates upward and outward. These beings could put on an Archangel Michael costume, but they would lack the essential element: the bright aura that results from living a life of Divine love. In this respect, clairvoyance helps us screen our friends in the physical and nonphysical worlds, and actually keeps us safe from harm.

4. "Evil" or punishment that this may be "wrong"

- *The fear:* Worrying that clairvoyance is the devil's work, and that God will punish you for sinning.

- *The truth:* This fear is often based on Old Testament quotes warning about wizards, mediums, and speaking with the dead. Yet, in the New Testament, we find Jesus and many others talking with the dead, and to angels as well. Saint Paul, in his letters to the Corinthians, exclaimed that we all have the gift of prophecy and that we should aspire to these spiritual gifts . . . as long as they're used with love.

    And that's the distinction, isn't it? The *Manual for Teachers* in *A Course in Miracles* says that psychic abilities can be used in service of the ego (which it says is the only devil in this world), or of the Holy Spirit. In other words, we can use clairvoyance for love or for fear. If you use this tool in the service of God and for healing purposes, there is nothing to fear. You will find that other peoples' judgments simply roll off of you.

5. Being ridiculed

- *The fear:* Being dubbed "crazy," "weird," "a know-it-all," or "too sensitive" . . . or dealing with the judgmental attitudes of fundamentalist relatives.

- *The truth:* You're probably a "lightworker" or an "Indigo Child"—that is, someone who feels compelled to make the world a better place from a spiritual perspective. Lightworkers, and their younger counterparts, the Indigo Children, very often feel like they're different or that they don't belong. When people tease you about your spiritual interests or gifts, it compounds that feeling even more. If you were teased during childhood, you may have unhealed emotional wounds associated with various types of ridicule. Ask your angels to intervene, and follow their guidance if they suggest that you seek professional help.

6. Taking inventory of your current life

- *The fear:* Being unprepared to make life changes if you see something you don't like about your life—that is, wanting to remain in denial.

- *The truth:* Clairvoyance may increase your awareness of parts of your life that aren't working. It's true that taking an inventory may increase your dissatisfaction in certain ways; however, taking an inventory of your relationships, career, health, or some other life area doesn't require you to make an immediate 180-degree turn and fix everything at once. Dissatisfaction is a powerful motivator toward taking steps to improve things. It inspires you to take up jogging, eat more healthfully, see a marriage counselor, and/or devise other methods for healing your life.

7. Seeing the future

- *The fear:* You may be wary of foreseeing planetary or social changes that are frightening.

- *The truth:* If you "see" these events, and you're absolutely certain that they aren't coming from your ego, then you'll have a better picture of your lightworker mission. You will be specifically guided as to how you can help the planet to avoid, or to cope with, these changes. For instance, you may be called on to pray for peace, to send healing energy, to anchor the light in various places, to teach other lightworkers, or to heal those who are affected by the changes. While such an assignment may seem daunting and intimidating, remember that you signed up for it prior to your incarnation . . . and God and the angels wouldn't have given you such a monumental assignment unless they knew that you could do it. They also provide you with full support along the way—as long as you ask for it and are open to receiving that help.

8. Too much responsibility

- *The fear:* Foreseeing a negative situation, you wonder, *Am I supposed to intervene?*

- *The truth:* Earth angels are usually just asked to pray about a situation unless it's a very special assignment, and if you *are* supposed to intervene or warn someone, you will be given very clear instructions about what to do.

9. Whether you can do it

- *The fear:* Worrying that you're an imposter, unqualified to be psychic or to perform spiritual healing; wondering whether you really have any angels, and if you do, whether you'll be able to make contact with them.

- *The truth:* Everyone feels like an imposter from time to time. Psychologists actually call this fear "The Imposter Syndrome." Research shows that some of the most competent, successful people are prone to experiencing this condition. It doesn't mean that you *are* an imposter; it just means that you're comparing your insides (which feel anxious in new situations) to everyone else's outsides (which appear to be calm, cool, and collected).

   The ego, or lower self, uses sleight-of-hand fears such as this one to distract us from remembering who we are and from working on our life purpose.

Past-Life Blocks to Clairvoyance

Sometimes the block to clairvoyance is rooted in our distant past. Even people who don't believe in reincarnation will agree that significant events in history are still affecting our world today. One of these events, as I mentioned earlier in the book, is the Spanish Inquisition, in which thousands of people were burned, hung, tortured, and robbed because they held spiritual beliefs or practices that were contrary to the reigning Church. The pain of that time still reverberates in the present day, as ancient echoes that cry, "Conform to accepted spiritual beliefs or suffer the consequences." Fear is the result, as well as "staying in the spiritual closet"—which leads you to keep your psychic abilities and spiritual beliefs a secret.

But how do you know if a past-life wound is blocking your clairvoyance? The signs include the following:

- You consider yourself nonvisually oriented—that is, you don't visualize easily, you rarely remember dreams, and you don't really focus on how people or things look.

- You've had few, if any, psychic visions.

- You feel tense or worried every time you think about opening up your clairvoyance.

- You have an undefined sense of anxiety about becoming psychic, as if you'd get into trouble or be punished by some individual or even by God.

- When you think about people being burned at the stake or hung, your body reacts strongly with chills, shivers, breathing changes, or tension.

In contrast, here are the signs that childhood experiences have blocked your clairvoyance:

- You saw angels, sparkling lights, or deceased people when you were a child.

- Your psychic visions diminished as you grew older.

- You are a highly sensitive person.

- You were teased for being "crazy," "evil," or "weird" as a child or adolescent.

- You worry what your family would think if you revealed your psychic gifts.

- You're afraid that, if you opened up psychically, you would make life changes that would disappoint or harm your family.

A past-life regression by a certified hypnotherapist, or via a vehicle such as my *Past-Life Regression with the Angels* audiotape is the most effective way to release these blocks. Your unconscious mind won't frighten you with memories that you can't handle, so please don't worry that a regression will overwhelm you.

Trying Too Hard

By far, the most common block to clairvoyance is trying too hard to see. As I touched on earlier, when we push or strain to do anything, we get blocked. That's because any type of strain stems from fear, which originates in the ego. The ego is 100 percent *not* psychic.

We try too hard when we fear, deep down, that we might not be able to achieve something, so we try to force it to happen. The underlying negativity, however, can undo hours of positive affirmations and manifestation efforts. The fear becomes a negative prayer that, unfortunately, attracts self-fulfilling prophecies.

Healing Psychic Blocks

Everyone has psychic blocks to one degree or another, so the point isn't to be completely clear of them. The point is to be *aware* of them, and deal with them promptly as they arise. Sometimes we become ashamed of our blocks, so we don't admit them to ourselves or others. Yet, blocks are nothing to be ashamed of. They are, however, areas of our life that require our attention.

A "healed healer" (to borrow the term from *A Course in Miracles*) isn't someone who is without issues. That would nearly be impossible in this world. A healed healer is someone who is aware of their issues and strives to avoid letting these issues interfere with their Divine life mission.

Nonetheless, we can heal and release issues that block us psychically. These healing techniques can also have markedly positive results on other life areas, in addition to clairvoyance:

— *Healing during sleep:* When we're sleeping, our skeptical mind is also asleep. That's why it's a perfect time to engage in spiritual healing. With the skeptical mind asleep, your ego can't block the angels from performing miraculous clearings on you. So, as soon as you're ready to open up your clairvoyance, ask your angels and anyone else in the spirit world with whom you work to come into your dreams. An example of how to ask is, "Archangel Raphael, I ask that you enter into my dreams tonight. Please send healing energy to my third eye, and heal away any fears that could be blocking my clairvoyance. Please help me to see clearly with my spiritual sight."

— *Cutting cords to family members:* If you realize that you're afraid of your mom's judgments about psychic abilities, for instance, you can use the cord-cutting techniques described earlier and direct them specifically toward cutting the cords of fear toward your mother. Repeat the process for any person (family member or otherwise) whom you worry about having a negative reaction to your clairvoyance. In addition, cut the cords with any individual from your past who ridiculed or punished you for being psychic.

— *Support from like-minded souls:* When I was preparing to "come out of the spiritual closet" and admit my clairvoyance publicly, I was naturally concerned about negative consequences. I was fortunate to become acquainted with a psychiatrist who was also admitting for the first time that he was a clairvoyant. Dr. Jordan Weiss was a university-trained internal medicine doctor, and a psychiatrist in private practice in Newport Beach, California. A recent head injury during an accident had opened up his third eye, and he found that he was able to see inside his patients' bodies. Dr. Weiss could also see the chakra systems and the negative emotions trapped inside these chakras. But he was afraid of openly admitting his clairvoyance, thereby risking his medical license and reputation.

We motivated, supported, and counseled each other with respect to going public with our clairvoyant gifts. We kept reminding each other that if we weren't true to ourselves, we really couldn't help our clients in the best possible way. Today, Dr. Weiss is completing his second book related to his psychic experiences as a psychiatrist.

I think *you* will also find it helpful to have the encouragement of someone else who's in a similar situation. Pray for such a person or a support group to come into your life, and you'll be guided to them. You can also consciously look for support at metaphysical meetings held at bookstores, New Thought churches such as Unity or Religious Science, psychic-development courses, or Internet bulletin boards related to the psychic arts.

— *Through sacred ceremony:* My husband, Steven Farmer, author of the book *Sacred Ceremony* (to be published by Hay House in 2002) has led healing ceremonies at many workshops. I've witnessed how these ceremonies help people release their psychic blocks. You can create your own sacred ceremony for the purpose of opening your clairvoyance. For example, write down a question for your angels, such as: "What is blocking my clairvoyance?" Then record whatever impressions you receive. Afterward, light a fire in your fireplace or an outdoor fire ring. Meditate for a moment on releasing the block written on the paper. When you truly feel ready to release it, throw the paper into the fire. You should feel a great sense of relief when you're done.

— *A past-life regression session or tape:* About half of the psychic blocks that I see in my audience members stem from their past-life wounds related to being psychic. As I mentioned earlier, it makes sense to go through a past-life regression to clear them. Most certified hypnotherapists are trained in giving past-life regressions. Your only task is to find a therapist with whom you feel comfortable, because your trust in the regressionist is key to your ability to let go and allow your unconscious memories to surface. Or, you can use a taped past-life regression such as my audio program (produced by Hay House) called *Past-Life Regression with the Angels.*

— *Positive affirmations:* I'm amazed by how many bright, knowledgeable metaphysicians complain to me that they're "just not visual." When I point out that this statement is a negative affirmation, they realize that these words are blocking their clairvoyance. Then, they begin using positive affirmations to describe what they desire instead of what they fear. "I am highly visual" and "I am profoundly clairvoyant" are examples of positive affirmations to say to yourself, even if you don't yet believe that they're true. Believe me—reality always catches up to your affirmed thoughts!

— *Calling on the angels of clairvoyance:* There are specialist angels for every situation, and psychic development is no exception. The "Angels of Clairvoyance" monitor and minister to our third-eye chakras, helping us develop spiritual sight. Mentally say, *"Angels of Clairvoyance, I call upon you now. Please surround my third eye with your healing and clearing energy. I ask for your help and assistance in fully opening my window of clairvoyance now. Thank you."* You will probably feel tingles and air-pressure changes in your head—especially between your two physical eyes—as the angels of clairvoyance do their healing work.

— *Lifestyle and clairvoyance:* There is a huge correlation between how well we treat our bodies and the vividness of our clairvoyance. Our visions are always clearer, more detailed, and more accurate when we're engaged in a consistently healthful lifestyle. Exercise, proper rest, getting outside regularly, eating a light plant-based diet, and avoiding toxins in food and beverages help us to be clearer channels of Divine communication.

After using one or more of the above healing processes, your clairvoyance should be noticeably brighter and clearer. In the next chapter, we'll put it all together, and look at how you can receive angel messages on behalf of yourself or another person.

---

[1]Stevenson, I. (1992). "A Series of Possibly Paranormal Recurrent Dreams." *Journal of Scientific Exploration*, Vol. 6, No. 3, pp. 281-289.

~ Receiving Messages ~ from Your Angels

My life purpose isn't to give angel readings and spiritual healings to clients. It's to teach *other people* how to give angel readings and spiritual healings to themselves and their clients. I always encourage my spiritual-counseling students to teach others—to create an ever-spreading ripple effect that increases the awareness that we *all* have angels, that we *all* can communicate with them, and that we *all* have spiritual gifts that we can use to help ourselves and the world.

In this chapter, you'll read some of the exact steps that I teach my psychic-development students so that you can give yourself and others angel readings.

How to Give an Angel Reading

An angel reading is similar to a psychic reading, except that you're directing the questions to guardian angels and spirit guides for the purpose of healing some life area, and/or for guidance about someone's life purpose.

It's best to give an angel reading to a person you don't know really well, someone who is open-minded and nonjudgmental. A new friend in a spiritual study group would be an ideal angel-reading partner. Still, you can definitely give an angel reading to a family member or old friend. It's just that your ego will scream at you: "You already knew this about this person!" If you can ignore the ego's rantings that "you're just making all of this up," you can give a reading to anyone, whether you know them or not.

Let's begin with a mutual angel reading, where you and another person are reading each other simultaneously. Begin your reading by saying a prayer to whomever you're aligned with spiritually, asking them:

> *"Please help me to be a clear channel of Divine communication. Please help me to clearly hear, see, know, and feel accurate and detailed messages that will bring blessings to my partner and myself. Please watch over this reading, and help me to relax and enjoy it. Thank you, and amen."*

Next, sit facing your partner. Then, both of you should take a metal object from your body, such as a watch, ring, necklace, belt buckle, hair clip, glasses, or car keys, and hand it to each other. Each of you should hold that metal object that you received from your partner in the hand that you normally don't write with. This is the hand where you receive energy—your "receptive hand."

Then, hold your partner's free hand with your free hand. Place your hands where they'll comfortably rest for the next few moment, such as on someone's knees or lap. Now, I'd like to take you both on a vacation, okay? Please close your eyes and breathe in and out very deeply. . . .

> *Mentally imagine that the two of you are in an exquisite purple pyramid that has magically transported you to a white sandy beach in Hawaii. The purple pyramid lands with a gentle plop on the sand and opens up, forming a natural blanket for the two of you. It is a perfect day in Hawaii, and since this is a completely isolated beach that's only accessible by boat or plane, you and your*

partner have complete privacy.

You feel the gentle summer breeze blowing across your skin and through your hair. You smell the delicious salt air, and hear the waves' melodic crash upon the shore. You feel a beam of sunlight dance warmly over the top of your head, as if it were going right in and illuminating the inside of your head and body.

Off in the distance, you notice a pod of dolphins swimming playfully in the ocean. You tune in to these dolphins, and you feel them send you a huge wave of Divine love energy. As your heart swells with warmth and gratitude for these beautiful dolphins and this perfect day on the beach, you realize that you're one *with the dolphins. And then this realization extends even further: you are* one *with all of the life in the ocean—including the sea turtles, the beautiful tropical fish, and . . . you're also one with the waves, the sand, and the sun.*

You realize that you're one with all of life, including your partner. And so you mentally affirm to your partner, "You and I are one . . . you and I are one . . . I am you . . . and you are me . . . you and I are one." You realize that this oneness that you share is real. Although you may look different on the outside, on the inside you and your partner truly do share one spirit, one light, one love. You mentally affirm to your partner, "One love . . . one love . . . one love."

As you revel in this knowingness, you also realize that you're one with all of the angels. As you scan your partner with your physical eyes closed and your spiritual sight wide open, imagine what it would be like if you could see your partner's angels in your mind's eye. What might they look like?

Do you see any angels that look like small cherubs? How about medium-sized angels? Really large ones? You might see these angels in full detail in your mind's eye, or as fleeting glimpses. Or, you might simply feel or know their presence.

As you continue to scan around your partner with your

spiritual sight, you might also notice some people who appear to be deceased loved ones. The beings who stand directly behind your partner are usually their deceased parents. Do you see a man or a woman standing directly behind your partner? If so, notice any distinguishing characteristics, such as anything unusual that they're wearing, eyeglasses, hairstyle, facial hair, eye color, or anything they're holding.

Next, scan around your partner's head and shoulders. Do you see anyone with light or gray hair who appears to have passed away when they were elderly? What other distinguishing features do you notice about them? How about anyone who looks like they passed away when they were middle-aged? Anyone who passed away young? Be aware of details relating to anyone who appears to you, not worrying about whether you're imagining this or not.

Do you see any animals around your partner? Any dogs or cats? Any small or large animals? What do you notice about their fur? Is it light, dark, or multicolored? Long, medium, or short?

As you scan around your partner one more time, notice any other angels, deceased loved ones, or animals that may be present. If one or more of these beings especially attracts your attention, tune in to them now by holding the intention of connecting with them.

Even if you don't see anyone around your partner, or you're unsure of yourself, you can still receive accurate messages from your partner's guides and angels that will bring blessings to him or her. As you breathe in and out deeply, hold the intention of having a mental conversation with these beings.

Now, mentally ask them, "What would you like me to know about my partner?" Repeat the question as you take note of impressions that come to you in response. Be aware of any thoughts, words, mental pictures, or feelings that come to you as you continue to ask the question, "What would you like me to know about my partner?" Don't try to force anything to happen. Simply trust that the *answers are coming to you now, and notice even the subtlest little thought, feeling, vision, or word that you mentally hear.*

Next, mentally ask your partner's guides and angels, "What message would you like me to tell my partner, from you?" Again, be cognizant of any impressions that come to you as thoughts, feelings, visions, or words. Don't judge or discount these impressions. Simply view them with detachment.

Then, mentally ask your partner's guides and angels, "Is there anything that you'd like to tell me?" Be sure, and breathe while you take heed of the answer.

Finally, mentally ask the guides and angels of your partner, "Is there anything else that you'd like me to tell my partner?" Again, listen for the response from many levels.

The most important part of giving an angel reading is having the courage to tell your partner everything that you received, even if you're unsure about the information or worry that it may offend this person (you can always pray for a diplomatic and loving way to deliver potentially offensive messages). While the angel messages may make no sense to you, they will likely make perfect sense to your partner. Spend the next few moments, then, sharing everything that you saw, felt, heard, or thought during your mutual angel reading.

How to Do Automatic Writing in a Safe, Controlled Manner

The angelic messages in this book and in *Angel Therapy* were received through the process of "automatic writing." This is a method that allows you to receive detailed messages from beyond. Sometimes people are afraid of automatic writing because they've heard stories about Earthbound spirits who come through these sessions pretending to be angels or master guides. But there are ways to absolutely protect yourself against such occurrences, as you'll read later on.

You can conduct automatic writing sessions with virtually anyone in the spirit world. It's a wonderful way to maintain and deepen relationships with deceased loved ones, and to heal unfinished business and grief. If your heart is hurting because you've lost loved ones, then you'll want to communicate with them through automatic writing.

You can use automatic writing to communicate with any of your deceased loved ones, even if they died before childbirth, as infants, or as toddlers. You can contact those who spoke different languages, or those who were retarded or mute—and you can even get in touch with your deceased pets. That's because our spirits communicate nonverbally, and then "translate" these messages into our own native language. You will probably notice, however, that your automatic writing transmissions involve words that normally aren't a part of your normal vocabulary. You may find that your handwriting changes, and that you can suddenly spell words that you weren't able to before (and vice versa).

Automatic writing can also assist you on your spiritual path. For instance, through this method, you can have conversations with God, your guardian angels, the ascended masters, and the archangels. You can ask your guardian angels, "What is your name?" and other queries. And you can ask the archangels and ascended masters to help you remember, and work on, your life's purpose.

You can also use automatic writing to connect with a spiritual mentor (see the full explanation of the Spiritual Mentorship Program in the chapter called "How to Recognize and Receive Divine Ideas and Profound Thoughts," starting on page 173).

You can handwrite your automatic writing message, or type it on a typewriter or word processor. If you're handwriting the message, you'll need at least four pieces of regular-sized paper, a firm writing surface, and a reliable writing utensil. It's a great idea to have some soothing music playing in the background, and to adopt a comfortable seating position.

Begin your automatic-writing sessions with a prayer. This is the one that I use before a session. It's based on my own spiritual beliefs, so you may want to rewrite the prayer to fit *your* belief system. I would never tell anyone whom to pray to, but I do offer this prayer as an example of a way to effectively ask for help:

> *"Dear God, Holy Spirit, Jesus, Archangel Michael, all of my guides, and all of my angels, I ask that you watch over this automatic writing session, and ensure that anyone who comes through is a positive and loving being. Please boost my ability to clearly hear, see, think, and feel your Divine communication. Please help me to accurately receive these messages, and to bring forth those that will bring blessings to me and to anyone who may read them. Thank you, and amen."*

Next, think about whomever you wish to connect with in Heaven. Mentally ask that being to have a conversation with you. You're going to pose a question, and then write the answer that you receive, in a question-and-answer format, similar to an interview. The most important thing to keep in mind while automatic writing is to be completely authentic. Write whatever impressions you get, even if you're unsure whether it's your imagination or not. If you're getting nothing, write that down. We begin with writing whatever is occurring, and then eventually it switches over and becomes authentic spiritual communication.

During the automatic-writing session, you may feel as if someone else is controlling your pen or pencil. As I mentioned earlier, your handwriting, vocabulary, and spelling style will likely change during the session. Don't let this frighten you, as fear can block Divine communication. Remember, you are safe and protected by God and Archangel Michael (who is the "bouncer angel," and won't let anyone come near you unless they have loving intentions). Your hand may also start to doodle little circles, which is the spirit world's way of greeting you and saying, "We're so happy to connect with you!" If the doodling continues for too long, tell them that you're happy to connect, too, but you'd appreciate it if they would switch over to communication that you can understand.

Your ego will probably have a field day during your automatic-writing session. It will scream at you, "You're just making this whole thing up!" If this happens, put the burden of proof that you actually are receiving authentic communications on the being with whom you're conversing. Ask the being, "How do I know that I'm not just making you up?" Their answer will likely convince you of the authenticity of your Divine conversation. If you're still not convinced, though, keep asking until you receive a message that puts your ego to rest. Or, ask the being to give you a physical sign, and then stop writing. Once you receive that physical sign, you'll feel more confident during your next session.

Now, let's begin by having you think of a question that you'd genuinely like answered. Mentally ask the spiritual being this question. Then, write the question at the top of the page while mentally repeating it. Be optimistic, holding the positive thought that you will be answered.

Write whatever impressions you receive through any of the four channels of Divine communication: thoughts, feelings, words, or visions. Then, ask another question and another answer, and so on.

When you're done writing to this being, you can switch to conversing with another being. When your communications are complete, be sure to thank everyone involved. The angels say that they love to give us messages, and that doing so is inherently rewarding to them because it's fulfilling God's will. Yet, when we thank our angels, our hearts fill with gratitude. And that warm feeling of appreciation is the "I love you" that we exchange with our celestial loved ones as a fitting finish to a love letter from Heaven.

~❧ Afterword ❧~

Letting Heaven Help You

Anyone can receive messages from their angels. In fact, we are all receiving messages from our angels . . . *right now.* If we can't understand these messages, we can ask our angels for assistance; we can also use some of the methods outlined in this book.

When you ask your angels for help or for answers, you aren't bothering them. The angels *want* to help us with every area of our lives because they want to bring peace to our planet one person at a time. If you think that you will feel more peaceful if you receive financial assistance, enter into a great love relationship, or secure a better job, then the angels are helping you with a sacred mission indeed. There is no request that is too trivial or monumental for the angels. You aren't pulling them off of a more important task when you ask for their assistance. After all, the number of angels available to help far exceeds the number of people making such requests. There are billions of angels who are "unemployed" and bored who would love to help you create a more meaningful and fruitful life.

Know that you deserve love, attention, and miraculous blessings from God and the angels. They love you unconditionally, no matter what mistakes you may have made in your life. You are just as special as anyone else who has ever lived. If it helps, remember that God made us all equally wonderful. To put yourself down is actually to put down God.

The ego tries to convince us that we don't warrant help or attention from Heaven, that we're somehow bad or unworthy. That is the ego's attempt to prevent us from remembering our true spiritual identity and power. Please don't listen to that voice, because it could delay you from working on your mission. And we need the fruits of your mission on this planet.

Allow yourself to be open to the messages from your angels. They won't tell you anything that you can't handle. The angels won't try to control your life, either. Their messages always help us to feel safer and happier, and make every aspect of our lives more meaningful.

You can call additional angels to your side (or to the side of your loved ones) simply by holding the thought that you'd like to be in contact with more angels. You can voice this response directly to God or to the angels. The result is the same, since the angels are extensions of God. They're literally God's thought-forms of love. Ask for as many angels as you'd like for yourself or another.

The angelic realm is filled with angels specializing in every human condition. You can ask for angels to help you find a new home, a soulmate, or to heal your body. There are angels who can help you with parenting, with school, and to be more motivated to exercise. The angels want to help you and give you messages, if only you'll let them. And the more that you allow Heaven to help you, the more resources you'll have to give back to the world.

When you develop the habit of getting your angels involved in every area of your life, you'll function like a member of a successful sports team. You aren't giving the angels complete responsibility for your life—you're simply passing the ball back and forth between your teammates, the angels. When you do this continually, life becomes so much simpler and more peaceful.

While suffering does create spiritual growth, contentment does so even more. You learn through peace, and more important, you can better teach your children and others when you're in a state of joyful relaxation. You don't need to suffer for growth! God certainly doesn't want you to endure pain, any more than you want your own children to do so.

By tuning in to the messages from your angels, you *can* help to create a peaceful world . . . one person at a time.

About the Author

Doreen Virtue, Ph.D., is a clairvoyant doctor of psychology who works with the angelic and elemental realms. She delivers their messages of guidance and inspiration through her writings and workshops. Her work includes the *Healing with the Angels* book, tape, and oracle cards; *Angel Therapy;* and *The Lightworker's Way.* Doreen is a frequent guest on television and radio talk shows—with appearances on *Oprah,* CNN, *The View, Good Morning America,* and other programs. Her work has been featured in major metropolitan newspapers and in national magazines.

A former psychotherapist who holds Ph.D., M.A., and B.A. degrees in counseling psychology, Doreen is a lifelong clairvoyant who came fully out of the "spiritual closet" and began openly teaching about angels following a brush with death in 1995. She gives workshops each weekend around the globe, including an Angel Therapy Practitioner (ATP Certification) course. For information about Doreen's workshop schedule, please visit her Website at: **www.AngelTherapy.com.**

Doreen welcomes submissions of true stories about Divine intervention; seeing angels, deceased loved ones, or ascended masters; or your angel experiences. Please submit your story (of any length) in the body of an e-mail to: **AngelStories@AngelTherapy.com.** Doreen's office will contact you if the story is selected for publication and ask you to specify whether you wish your real name to be used or to be published anonymously.

⁓ Hay House Titles ⁓
of Related Interest

Books

The Experience of God: *How 40 Well-Known*
Seekers Encounter the Sacred, by Jonathan Robinson

The Indigo Children: *The New Kids Have Arrived,*
by Lee Carroll and Jan Tober

In the Palm of Your Hand: *Practical Palmistry for Career and*
Relationship Success, by Liz Gerstein

Mirrors of Time: *Using Regression for Physical, Emotional,*
and Spiritual Healing, by Brian L. Weiss M.D.
(includes past-life regression CD)

Sacred Ceremony: *How to Create Ceremonies for Healing, Transitions,*
and Celebrations, by Steven D. Farmer, Ph.D.

Visionseeker: *Shared Wisdom from the Place of Refuge,*
by Hank Wesselman, Ph.D.

You Can Heal Your Life, by Louise L. Hay

Audio Programs

Angels and Spirit Guides: How to Call Upon Your Angels and Spirit Guide for Help, by Sylvia Browne

Angels! Angels! Angels!, by Denise Linn

Invocation of the Angels, by Joan Borysenko, Ph.D.

Mystical Power: Talks on Spirituality and Modern Life, by Marianne Williamson

Understanding Your Angels and Meeting Your Guides, by John Edward

All of the above are available at your local bookstore, or may be ordered through Hay House, Inc.

We hope you enjoyed this Hay House book. If you would like to receive a free catalog featuring additional Hay House books and products, or if you would like information about the Hay Foundation, please contact:

Hay House, Inc.
P.O. Box 5100
Carlsbad, CA 92018-5100

(760) 431-7695 or **(800) 654-5126**
(760) 431-6948 (fax) or **(800) 650-5115 (fax)**
www.hayhouse.com

Published and distributed in Australia by:
Hay House Australia Pty. Ltd. • 18/36 Ralph St. • Alexandria NSW 2015
Phone: 612-9669-4299 • *Fax:* 612-9669-4144 • www.hayhouse.com.au

Published and distributed in the United Kingdom by:
Hay House UK, Ltd. • Unit 62, Canalot Studios
222 Kensal Rd., London W10 5BN • *Phone:* 44-20-8962-1230
Fax: 44-20-8962-1239 • www.hayhouse.co.uk

Published and distributed in the Republic of South Africa by:
Hay House SA (Pty), Ltd., P.O. Box 990, Witkoppen 2068
Phone/Fax: 2711-7012233 • orders@psdprom.co.za

Distributed in Canada by: Raincoast
9050 Shaughnessy St., Vancouver, B.C. V6P 6E5
Phone: (604) 323-7100 • *Fax:* (604) 323-2600

Sign up via the Hay House USA Website to receive the Hay House online newsletter and stay informed about what's going on with your favorite authors. You'll receive bimonthly announcements about: Discounts and Offers, Special Events, Product Highlights, Free Excerpts, Giveaways, and more!
www.hayhouse.com